INTEGRATING
PSYCHOLOGY
AND **FAITH**

INTEGRATING PSYCHOLOGY AND FAITH

Models for Christian Engagement

**PAUL MOES
AND BLAKE RIEK**

Baker Academic
a division of Baker Publishing Group
Grand Rapids, Michigan

© 2023 by Paul E. Moes and Blake M. Riek

Published by Baker Academic
a division of Baker Publishing Group
Grand Rapids, Michigan
www.bakeracademic.com

Printed in the United States of America

All rights reserved. No part of this publication may be reproduced, stored in a retrieval system, or transmitted in any form or by any means—for example, electronic, photocopy, recording—without the prior written permission of the publisher. The only exception is brief quotations in printed reviews.

Library of Congress Cataloging-in-Publication Data
Names: Moes, Paul, 1955– author. | Riek, Blake, 1979– author.
Title: Integrating psychology and faith : models for Christian engagement / Paul Moes and Blake Riek.
Description: Grand Rapids, Michigan : Baker Academic, a division of Baker Publishing Group, 2023. | Includes bibliographical references and index.
Identifiers: LCCN 2023014295 | ISBN 9781540964755 (paperback) | ISBN 9781540966865 (casebound) | ISBN 9781493442973 (ebook) | ISBN 9781493442980 (pdf)
Subjects: LCSH: Psychology—Religious aspects—Christianity. | Psychology and religion. | Christianity—Psychology. | Christianity and other religions.
Classification: LCC BF51 .M64 2023 | DDC 248.401/9—dc23/eng/20230701
LC record available at https://lccn.loc.gov/2023014295

Scripture quotations are from THE HOLY BIBLE, NEW INTERNATIONAL VERSION®, NIV® Copyright © 1973, 1978, 1984, 2011 by Biblica, Inc.® Used by permission. All rights reserved worldwide.

Baker Publishing Group publications use paper produced from sustainable forestry practices and post-consumer waste whenever possible.

23   24   25   26   27   28   29   7   6   5   4   3   2   1

We dedicate this book to our students,
who regularly challenge and inspire us
with good questions,
and to our families,
who support us in our
professional and personal lives.

Contents

Acknowledgments

The idea for this book arose, in part, from both of us having taught a course called Psychology and Religion, which serves as the capstone course for Calvin University's psychology major. This course was initially developed by our former colleague Glenn Weaver, and he served as a mentor for each of us as we began to teach the course. Glenn's influence can be felt throughout this book, and we are extremely grateful for his work and friendship. We also gratefully acknowledge the invaluable critique and feedback of the manuscript provided by Glenn Weaver and Heather Looy. We also wish to express our gratitude for the financial support provided by Calvin University and the Calvin Center for Christian Studies for the completion of this book. Finally, we want to thank our wives, Phyllis Moes and Melanie Riek, for their support throughout this project.

Preface

A student who is devoutly religious and wants to study psychology may receive a variety of reactions from friends, family, and faculty. Some of our students over the years have been warned by friends and family to be careful with psychology because it contains secular viewpoints that are perceived to conflict with religious belief. On the other end of the spectrum, some may be told that psychological science is empirical and objective and should be trusted over religious belief. Others may be told that psychology and religious belief are just different ways of expressing similar truths. Or perhaps students are encouraged to pursue both their faith and their interest in psychology but to keep them somewhat separate.

These are just some of the possible ways of viewing the intersection of religious belief and the field of psychology. Sorting out the underlying assumptions and implications of these different approaches can be confusing. The goal of this book is to help clarify these issues.

Rather than just listing different approaches to faith and psychology, we hope to help readers understand the reasoning behind the different approaches. To that end, the first half of this book is dedicated to covering important concepts, such as views of science, human nature, psychology, and religion. While these are often seen as abstract philosophical concepts, these principles lay the groundwork for the different approaches to integrating faith and psychology. For example, a person's philosophy of science will directly impact what types of knowledge they see as valid sources of information. In addition, a person's view of religion will clearly have a large influence on the role they believe Scripture should have in understanding psychological concepts. The second half of the book builds on these ideas and outlines different models of integration, while evaluating the pros and cons of each approach. Of course, these models are not exhaustive, and variations exist within the models. But we hope these examples will give readers a lay of the land and perhaps help them identify their own approach to integrating faith and psychology.

While the primary audience of this book is Christians who may be interested in the field of psychology, we also hope this text can be useful for non-Christians who are curious about the different ways faith can be coupled with psychological science. Christian approaches to psychology are not monolithic, and hopefully seeing the diversity of approaches can help non-Christian psychologists find common ground with Christian scientists and practitioners of psychology.

Several excellent books and articles published over the years address these issues. Why one more? For one, we believe that the conversation regarding the nature of psychological science always requires review and renewal. In addition, new ideas and findings from diverse fields such as neuroscience, organizational psychology, evolutionary psychology, and clinical practice continue to raise complex questions for persons of faith. We do not attempt to provide complete answers to these questions. Instead, we explore ways that various Christian scholars and practitioners have approached them. Addressing this vast landscape would require a much longer book. Our goal was to write a relatively brief book that would summarize and evaluate foundational issues and contemporary applications. If this book is being used as part of a course on integration, we encourage the use of additional reading material to expand on and apply the foundational ideas presented here. We encourage readers to continue their exploration of their own worldview, the complex issues within the field, and how to relate their worldview to psychology.

Paul Moes
Blake Riek

PART 1

PHILOSOPHICAL FOUNDATIONS

"Where are you coming from?" This question is especially frequent among first-year college students who are curious about another student's origins. Of course, a person's origin includes their previous physical location, such as their home city, region, or country. However, the question often implies, "What shaped you as a person or influenced the views you hold right now?" We are shaped by our physical surroundings, but we are also molded by our teachers, religious leaders, parents, peers, social media, and personal experiences. It's rare to fully recognize these formative influences on our attitudes and values until we step into a different context. We also fail to notice how much our attitudes and values influence how we interpret new information.

As psychologists, we have often asked a similar question about other psychologists: "Where are they coming from?" We ask the question because we are curious about what formed their views, which may be quite different from our own. How and why did they arrive at such a different approach when we are looking at the same reality and may even share some common education? This book focuses on the different approaches Christian psychologists have used when relating faith to psychology. But it's not enough just to describe these approaches; it's also helpful to know why adherents to a particular approach believe what they believe. You may not agree with the basic belief system of another person, but once you know what that system is, you can better appreciate why they came to a certain conclusion. It can also be helpful to know why *you* believe what you believe and what formed those views. Therefore, the first part of the book examines some of the philosophical, religious, and personal beliefs that shape a person's approach to science in general and psychological science in particular.

1

Worldviews and Natural Science Beliefs

Truthiness: . . . the belief in what you feel to be true rather than what the facts will support.

Stephen Colbert, *The Colbert Report*

Feel facts: things that aren't technically true, but they feel true.

Kate McKinnon, *Saturday Night Live*

Most students of psychology accept that psychology is defined as the science of behavior and mental processes, and they embrace the idea that psychology seeks to learn the truth about behavior. But as the two tongue-in-cheek quotations above suggest, truth is not always easy to identify. This chapter focuses on diverse views concerning the nature of scientific knowledge and how worldviews influence those views.

The central purpose of this book is to describe various models for how faith can be related to the science and practice of psychology. While we address diverse philosophical positions and perspectives, the primary focus is on the implications of Christian faith. An additional goal is to describe how and why individuals arrive at the various models. We hope to show that individuals embrace certain models because of many factors, including but not limited to their views about science, their religious or theological views, their views about people and society, their cultural background, and even their personal experiences. Collectively, these factors lead to a perspective that can simply be called a worldview.

A Word about Worldviews

The term *worldview* has been defined by many Christian[1] and secular[2] authors, and its formal use has a long history.[3] While not everyone agrees on a single definition of the term, engineering professor Ken Funk has provided a succinct summary. He defines worldview as "the set of beliefs about fundamental aspects of reality (i.e., human nature, existence of God) that ground and influence all one's perceiving, thinking, knowing, and doing."[4] You might think of your worldview as the lens through which you view the world; you might also call it your personal philosophy of life about big questions (e.g., the existence of God, the nature of reality) or your basic value system. Funk adds that a worldview includes a collection of beliefs or assumptions that are interrelated, and they may or may not be explicit or fully articulated. Even if we are not fully aware of our assumptions, we can observe our behavior to understand the nature of our belief systems. Of course, human nature being what it is, we are not always perfectly consistent with our actions, and sometimes we hold two different perspectives that are contradictory without being aware of the inconsistency.

Consider the following scenarios.

Scenario 1: A Black pastor of a predominantly Black church was alarmed by recent marches for racial justice that were prompted by a police shooting of an unarmed Black man. The marches started peacefully, but some marchers became violent, resulting in many arrests.

---

1. Wolters, *Creation Regained*, 2.
2. Koltko-Rivera, "Psychology of Worldviews," 3.
3. Naugle, *Worldview*.
4. Funk, "What Is a Worldview?"

The pastor believes in the cause of racial justice and stood with the protesters. He understands their anger and frustration and feels that the police contribute to systemic racism and that the police response to protests made the situation worse. He feels that Christians should be active in society by working for cultural change. However, as a devout Christian, he is disturbed by the violence because he believes that the gospel requires nonviolence as well as justice. A white suburban mother of three was also alarmed by the protests. She supports racial justice, but she believes the violence needs to be stopped with strong measures. As a devout Christian, she feels that the Bible teaches us to obey earthly authorities. She understands that there are some racially biased individuals but believes that society should prosecute "bad apples" in the police force and not blame the system.

Both individuals find support for their positions on social media, and sophisticated algorithms on these platforms feed them opinions and stories that support their ideas about this situation. Surprisingly, when similar protests occur a few weeks later—but this time involving right-wing extremists and white nationalists—the two individuals shift their responses. Now the pastor wants the protests to be handled with strong measures. While the suburban mother is also disturbed by these groups, she feels it is their right to protest.

Scenario 2: Samuel, an undergraduate student at a private, religiously affiliated university, recently bragged to friends that he had hooked up with several female students. Later, when his friends were discussing Samuel's behavior, Tony stated that this is "just what guys do." He has learned recently from studying evolutionary psychology that men evolved differently from women and that Samuel's behavior is just a product of sexual selection. Connie is appalled at Tony's statement, and, as a very religious person, she feels that Samuel's actions are wrong because there are absolute moral rules that should not be broken. Sarah also believes that Samuel's behavior is wrong but that it is not her place to impose her religious beliefs on him because each person needs to decide their own moral path.

Scenario 3: As a strong Catholic raised in a very traditional Hispanic household, Felipe has always believed that men and women should adhere to traditional gender roles. While taking a behavioral neuroscience class in college, he readily embraced research showing that men and women develop somewhat different brains. In addition, he endorses evolutionary psychologists who suggest that sexual selection creates very different gender-based behavior patterns. At the same time, Felipe rejects biological evidence suggesting that same-sex attraction and gender dysphoria may be influenced by biological factors. He feels that such research was conducted by scientists with a very antibiblical and socially progressive bias and that they were misguided or just plain wrong. Besides, it's the soul that really counts when making moral choices, so even if the body is "dysfunctional," a person's soul can still make correct moral choices.

Mary took the same behavioral neuroscience class as Felipe. She feels that the research showing biological differences between men and women was terribly biased. She also suggests that evolutionary psychology ideas about sexual selection are not scientific findings or even harmless theories about human behavior but rather dangerous assaults on the struggle for gender equality. However, she is very interested in studies suggesting that homosexuality and gender dysphoria are the result of biological factors during early development.

Jordan, a third student in the class, simply does not understand the reactions of Felipe and Mary. Jordan feels that these findings are objective realities and that opinion and bias have no place in the process. We should just receive fact-based information for what it is and accept reality.

It is clear from these stories that individuals quickly and almost automatically interpret situations and ideas based on long-standing assumptions and views. Each person sees the same event or information, but each reacts very differently based on their worldview. While all the individuals can articulate reasons for their positions, it is likely that they are not fully conscious of how they arrived at these positions. This becomes especially evident when we consider some potential inconsistencies in their positions. Why should the violence of white nationalists be viewed differently than the violence of social justice advocates? Why should biological influences be valid predictors of gender differences but not of gender dysphoria? More seems to be influencing their reactions than a set of conscious, well-reasoned arguments or hard "facts." Even when people are more consistent (like Jordan in the third scenario), they still have preconceived notions about the nature of morality, culture, and science. If we engage in some careful self-reflection, most of us would realize that we bring assumptions and various levels of consistency to the way we view situations. People are not always fully aware of all aspects of their worldview because a worldview develops gradually through a lifetime of cultural influence, personal experience, religious education, social media influence, and so on. Whether we should allow worldviews to shape ideas in psychology or should work to minimize or eliminate their impact is the focus of this book.

Why do worldviews exist, and why do they have such a powerful influence on our perceptions and actions? Psychologist Mark Koltko-Rivera provides one explanation from terror management theory. This theory suggests that worldviews help us make sense of the world in the face of threats to our well-being. While supporting evidence for this theory has been mixed,[5] Koltko-Rivera believes that managing threats may be only part of the reason for having a worldview. He postulates that it should really be called "reality management theory" and suggests that "people will defend their [culturally dominant] worldview whenever they are in a state of insecurity."[6] He goes on to state that "reality is not interpretable 'as is,' without some hermeneutic framework; culturally transmitted worldviews give a sense of coherence to all aspects of life and reality."[7] Koltko-Rivera also argues that worldviews are different from cognitive structures or schemas in that they cannot be falsified with data or observation because they often deal with issues that cannot be directly tested with evidence. Scientific theories are also different from worldviews because theories are presumably tied more directly to observation.[8] In summary, worldviews help make a very complex world sensible and understandable in the face of incomplete information, uncertainties, and even threats.

5. See the review by Burke, Martens, and Faucher, "Two Decades of Terror Management Theory."
6. Koltko-Rivera, "Psychology of Worldviews," 20.
7. Koltko-Rivera, "Psychology of Worldviews," 20.
8. Of course, theories have the potential to be influenced by worldviews, but they are still distinct in many ways.

This explanation of worldview underscores how essential world-views might be when we attempt to interpret the science and the practice of psychology. As with all areas of study, knowledge gained from psychological science is inherently incomplete. There is simply no way to adequately capture all the specific influences on behavior or the infinite variety of interrelationships among these influences. Therefore, scientific findings about people almost always require us to fill in the knowledge gaps by providing some type of hermeneutic (interpretation structure) and coherence to make sense of the data. For example, in scenario 3, everyone is dealing with the same data, but they come to very different conclusions. Herein lies the crux of the issue: Is it possible to fill in the gaps of knowledge and strive for a completely objective psychological science based on observable facts, or are social sciences—and perhaps all sciences—inherently subjective and constructed? This question can be answered in various ways, and many levels of the scientific process (e.g., theory building versus larger worldview assumptions) need to be considered when addressing the issue. These will be examined in subsequent chapters. However, to better understand how these questions can be addressed, we need to first understand different elements of worldview.

The Wide World of Worldviews

Worldviews can involve narrow questions about our present situation and large, existential questions about meaning and existence. Philosopher Clément Vidal outlines six major elements related to the big issues in life, while Ken Funk outlines seven elements. Here is a paraphrase and consolidation of their two lists—along with additional questions related to these elements:

1. Where do things come from (cosmology)? Was the world, along with all living creatures, created instantly or gradually by an all-knowing being, or do the laws of physics govern the origin and continuation of the world without a larger purpose or meaning?

2. What is the nature of reality (metaphysics or ontology)? Is nature guided by random events or some cohesive patterns or physical laws? Are humans comprised of only material substance, or is there more?

3. What is true or false (epistemology)? Can we be certain about knowledge? How should we obtain knowledge?

4. Is there purpose (teleology)? Is there a purpose for the existence of matter? Do humans—collectively or individually—have a purpose? Is there some planned outcome for all of life?

5. What are human beings (anthropology)? Are we just flesh and blood, or are we body and soul? Are humans prone toward goodness or evil? Are we determined by physical forces, or do we have free will?

6. What is right or wrong (axiology)? Do universal moral principles exist, or is right and wrong determined by natural, cultural, or situational circumstances?[9]

As you read through this list, perhaps your eyes have glazed over from such abstract ideas, or perhaps you feel that these ideas are not very relevant for your daily life, or perhaps you are noncommittal about many of these concepts (i.e., "I just don't know" or "I'm agnostic"). However, if you think back to the three scenarios presented at the outset, you can see that a person's view about knowledge or truth, human beings, or right and wrong can have a significant impact on their reaction to an issue. Whether or not we are conscious of these big questions, they influence how we think about personal and social issues as well as natural and social science.

The remainder of this chapter focuses on cosmology, ontology, and epistemology, with some mention of teleology, worldview elements that shape our view of science—primarily natural science but also the scientific process of observation and hypothesis testing that could be applied to any area of study. The following chapter focuses on elements that are unique to social science—namely, teleology, anthropology, and axiology.

9. Vidal, "What Is a Worldview?," 4–6; and Funk, "What Is a Worldview?"

Origins (Cosmology) and Reality (Ontology)

The origin of things and the nature of reality are often the starting points for many of the other questions. A naturalistic worldview would state that everything (including the universe) has a natural cause and that there are no supernatural aspects to reality. Therefore, things like purpose and morality must have natural causes. However, if you believe that God or some other intelligent being created and sustains the universe and everything in it, then you have a very different idea about the nature of reality as well as issues such as truth, purpose, and morality. If God creates and sustains the universe, then perhaps some aspects of reality are unknowable by humans, since God himself is not fully knowable—which might diminish interest in science for some. However, as Malcolm Jeeves and Thomas Ludwig point out, belief in God does not rule out scientific investigation. In fact, there is a long history of strong support for scientific investigation by persons of faith.[10] Likewise, Stanton Jones argues that a Christian worldview promotes interest in science because it stresses the importance of the physical world (i.e., God's good creation) and the expectation of regularity in that world.[11] Nonetheless, as we will see in subsequent chapters, persons of faith have varying degrees of apprehension about aspects of science because science sometimes draws inferences about origins and about the ultimate nature of reality that could potentially be in conflict with Scripture.

Ways of Knowing (Epistemology)

Views about epistemology (knowledge) shape how accepting we might be of science as well as the type of science we might conduct. If you are unfamiliar with philosophy of science questions, then you may assume that all investigators conduct science in the same way and have the same attitudes about what science is and what it does. However, not all individuals seeking knowledge of the world go about it the same way. Therefore, a brief primer on the philosophy of science is

10. Jeeves and Ludwig, *Psychological Science and Christian Faith*, 20.
11. Jones, "Integration View," 112.

in order. Joseph Ponterotto provides a succinct overview of the major approaches to science, which we summarize here.[12]

Positivism. This approach suggests that the world is objectively knowable (i.e., "I'm positive this is true") and that we can come to know absolute truth through careful observation and measurement (empiricism). This approach emphasizes quantitative (i.e., data gathering) methods using carefully controlled experimentation and the hypothetico-deductive method. This basic process, taught in most research methods classes, involves the development of a testable hypothesis, careful manipulation and control of conditions, and a process of logical deduction that allows a researcher to confirm or disconfirm the hypothesis. If the findings are replicated by other researchers, then we can use these well-established facts to develop causal laws that govern all aspects of the universe. These laws are not only discoverable, but they are also all anyone needs to know to fully understand all aspects of reality. Most individuals who adhere strongly to this position suggest that the social sciences should follow this approach typically used in the natural sciences. You can see hints of this view being expressed by Jordan in scenario 3.

Postpositivism. In recent decades, several investigators have become dissatisfied with strict positivism and have moved toward postpositivism. Perhaps the most common form of postpositivism, critical realism, accepts that there is an objective reality that can be discovered but that humans always understand that reality imperfectly.[13] Because of the inherently limited or even flawed nature of human perception and because of the overwhelming complexity of the natural and social worlds, we can never fully capture reality. This position suggests that data does not prove or completely verify a theory or hypothesis; we can only falsify a theory. The philosopher Karl Popper provided an example using swans.[14] If we hypothesize that all swans are white, observing a million white swans does not verify the hypothesis because we need to find only one black swan to falsify the theory. Therefore, this approach values empirical research, the hypothetico-deductive method, and an

---

12. Ponterotto, "Qualitative Research," 126.
13. For an overview, see Archer et al., *Critical Realism.*
14. Ponterotto, "Qualitative Research," 129.

objective approach to science, but it is much more tentative than positivism about the potential for science to arrive at absolute truth. One subtype of critical realism is called critical naturalism. It distinguishes between natural and social sciences, suggesting that social science calls for methods distinct from those of natural science because it needs to account for freely chosen behavior.

Constructivism-interpretivism. This approach stands in sharp contrast to the other positions because it proposes that there is not one objective reality but rather multiple valid realities—based on the minds of the people perceiving those realities. Therefore, the way a researcher interprets the world is essential to the process, and the approach embraces a form of relativism by assuming multiple valid realities.

As Ponterotto suggests, this approach goes back to the philosopher Immanuel Kant. "According to Hamilton (1994, p. 63), Kant's position was that 'human perception derives not only from evidence of the senses but also from the mental apparatus that serves to organize the incoming sense impressions' and that 'human claims about nature cannot be independent of inside-the-head processes of the knowing subject.'"[15]

This approach favors qualitative research, in which there is greater interaction between the researcher and the object of investigation. In this scenario, the researcher is not just a passive and objective observer of the facts but is actively shaping the interaction and interpreting the phenomenon in question. Some researchers who will be described in later chapters favor this more interpretive approach but do not necessarily believe that there are multiple valid realities. Most individuals embracing this approach still adhere to peer reviews of findings and the elimination of individual bias—but they allow greater influence of group or cultural perspectives. Ponterotto observes that some researchers believe this approach should be applied to the social sciences but that positivist or postpositivist approaches are more well suited for natural science.[16] While not engaging in a formal research process, the two individuals described in scenario 1 mirror elements of this

15. Ponterotto, "Qualitative Research," 129. In this quotation, Ponterotto quotes from Hamilton, "Traditions, Preferences, and Postures," 63.
16. Ponterotto, "Qualitative Research," 129.

approach in that they see the same event through a very deliberate interpretive framework.

Critical-ideological. This approach suggests that reality is completely constructed by social forces. These forces often lead to a "type of truth" that allows for the powerful control of one group by another. The goal of the investigator is not to discover objective reality but to develop a narrative that aids groups who are oppressed by forces beyond their control. This approach favors the exclusive use of qualitative methods, is often used in gender or cross-cultural studies, and is rarely directly applied to any aspect of natural science (with the possible exception of potential neurological differences between men and women). You can see hints of this view in Mary's response in scenario 3, when she suggests that studies showing brain differences between men and women negatively impact the fight for gender equality.

Renee Schwartz and Norma Lederman conducted a qualitative study of some of these attitudes using a cross section of natural science researchers.[17] They found a range of attitudes about the tentative nature of scientific knowledge, the essential nature of empirical observation versus inference and logical analysis, the role of subjectivity and creativity in science, and the role of cultural and social values in science. While some of the respondents in their survey clearly expressed a very strict positivist approach, a sizable portion also saw room for inference, subjectivity, and cultural influence in at least some aspects of natural science work. The point of their study was to show, as we stated earlier, that scientists are not unanimous in their perspectives on science.

Faith, Worldviews, and Science

How does faith impact these large worldview questions and ultimately a person's view of science? The answer is quite varied. As described earlier, a person's view of cosmology and ontology is very dependent on religious orientation. Another large question that distinguishes most persons of faith from nonreligious scientists involves teleology or purpose. While differences exist among religious groups in how

17. Schwartz and Lederman, "What Scientists Say."

to apply this idea in science, most religions claim that some force, guiding principle, or God creates, sustains, and/or guides the natural world. This implies some form of ultimate purpose for existence as well as some form of ultimate end goal for the universe. If this is the case, how do we square it with physical or causal laws that dictate all activity and therefore have no purpose or end goal? For example, how can we say that a hurricane was an "act of God" when we can also describe and predict the physical factors that brought about such an event? As several authors have noted, many religious explanations concerning the natural world can result in a "God of the gaps" approach to the natural world.[18] In other words, any time there are gaps in our scientific knowledge, that is where we plug in a God explanation. The concern is that as we discover more and more about the natural world, God—or any religious explanation—begins to vanish entirely. While a full discussion of this issue is beyond the scope of this book, we should note that this apparent contradiction between naturalistic and divine explanations for the world is something that causes many persons of faith to struggle with science in general. For a full discussion of how some persons of faith have grappled with this issue, see Wayne Frair and Gary Patterson's *Science and Christianity: Four Views.*

Space does not permit an analysis of how various religious groups around the world have responded to the questions about the nature of knowledge and the basic nature of natural science, so we will focus on how Christians have responded. Not surprisingly, Christians have varied a great deal in their approach to science. Yet it is safe to say that virtually all persons who embrace a religious faith—regardless of that religion—generally do not embrace a strict or exclusive positivist approach, since a logical conclusion of positivism is that all truth is guided by observation. Therefore, belief in a God or spirits, life after death, spiritual change, and so on would not be considered valid truths but be considered simply speculations of the mind. However, some Christians in science believe that the positivist approach is appropriate but only when applied to certain aspects of the natural world and that it should be considered separate from larger ques-

18. For a good overview, see Berg, "Leaving Behind the God-of-the-Gaps."

tions about meaning and purpose. Others feel that positivism is in opposition to faith because the approach implies that the only way to established truth is through observation. Some have gravitated toward a postpositivist view of science because they feel it allows room for the influence of worldview or even faith perspectives when doing science. Still others have embraced either a critical naturalism position (i.e., social science requiring a different method) or something bordering on a constructivist view as being more compatible with a faith perspective because these allow their faith perspective to be applied more intentionally to their scientific work.[19] These psychologists also tend to favor more qualitative research in psychology. While the critical-ideological approach has not been embraced by many Christian groups, some have argued that Christians should be more forceful in applying a biblical worldview to all areas of science. These same individuals suggest that many in the feminist movement, for example, have long promoted a certain perspective within science, so promoting a Christian or biblical agenda within science or applied disciplines is equally legitimate.

The variety of views concerning science and certainty raises questions about how one might evaluate claims of "truth" from science. The same question could easily be raised about truth claims from philosophy or religion. Christian psychologist David Entwistle summarizes the intellectual humility that he feels is necessary to avoid the overconfidence of some positivists but also the relativism at the other end of the continuum: "At best, we can humbly try to evaluate our beliefs carefully enough to arrive at a contingent certainty; that is, if our assumptions are correct, and if we discern a coherent epistemology, and if we apply our epistemic methodologies consistently, then we can be tentatively certain about our conclusions. To hope for (or worse, to claim) more than that is to assert a god-like quality which frail, fallen, and finite creatures cannot attain."[20]

---

19. Some Christian psychologists lean toward a more constructivist view because they view the mind of the observer as significantly shaping the social science process. However, most would not fully embrace the more relativistic perspective that there are multiple truths.

20. Entwistle, *Integrative Approaches to Psychology and Christianity*, 97.

Reflections and Conclusions

As we will see in subsequent chapters, these worldview questions—whether we are conscious of them or not—influence how we view both natural and social science. As we explore models of the relationship between faith and psychology in chapters 5–8, we will see how these foundational questions influence the model one chooses. But it is also time for a bit of self-reflection. Where do you fit on the continuum of scientific attitudes? Why do you think that way, and what factors influenced you to gravitate toward that view? Answering such questions will help you determine the approach to psychology that you favor and help you understand how you got there. It may also help you see inconsistencies in your worldview and allow you to update your worldview to be more consistent.

QUESTIONS FOR DISCUSSION

1. What are some social, religious, and intellectual influences that have shaped your worldview? Is your worldview cohesive, fully articulated, and well established, or is it unclear, unconscious, or in development?

2. Where would you place yourself on the continuum of big question worldview positions? How have these positions influenced your view of natural science and psychology?

3. Is there a way to determine what is true? What is your own method for trying to establish truth, and how certain can you or should you be?

2

Worldviews about Human Nature

For you will certainly carry out God's purpose, however you act, but
it makes a difference to you whether you serve like Judas or like John.

C. S. Lewis, *The Problem of Pain*

If you think the issues of worldview and natural science discussed in the
first chapter were deep and complex, just wait until we discuss human
beings! A few years ago, colleagues of ours presented a seminar on
God's providence in the light of natural laws. In other words, how does
God work out his plans in relation to the natural order of the world he
created? A psychologist in the audience suggested that, even though
this is a difficult issue, it is relatively simple compared to the challenge
of adding human agency (free will) into the mix. In other words, how
can God have a plan for each individual when the personal decisions of
billions of people impact the outcome of human history? Let us give a
simple example of the dilemma. One of the authors (Paul Moes) moved
to his current location several years ago. He wasn't actively looking
for a new position but happened—quite by "accident"—to see an ad

for his present position. Several years later, when discussing this with his daughter-in-law, they mused that had he not seen that ad and had he not decided to move his family, his sons would not have met their spouses and his grandchildren would not have been born! Christians routinely speak of God having a plan and knowing of the existence of each person before the creation of the world, yet a free choice made all the difference in the outcome.

This is just one of the many dilemmas in trying to square worldview perspectives with the field of psychology. Questions about natural laws, embodiment, predictability, human agency, good and evil, responsibility, relationality, meaning, purpose, and so on certainly make the science of behavior a complicated endeavor relative to issues faced within the natural sciences. The perspective that someone takes on these issues will also impact the way they approach the field of psychology.

Continuing the themes presented in the first chapter, we turn here to worldview perspectives that have a direct impact on how we view human beings and how these views might impact the model of faith and psychology integration we might select. Remember from chapter 1 that anthropology relates to our view of humans and focuses on questions such as, Are we just flesh and blood, or are we body and soul? Are humans prone toward goodness or evil? Are we determined by physical forces, or do we have free will? You may notice that these questions overlap with those related to other worldview positions, such as ontology (i.e., what we are made of and how we function), teleology (i.e., agency and purpose), and axiology (i.e., moral direction). We will also touch once again on epistemology as it relates to studying human beings. As we attempt to describe each of the main questions of anthropology, you will see that many of the questions overlap and that a person's view on one question often coincides with certain positions on other questions.

What Am I? Issues of Embodiment and Relationality

Asking the "What am I?" question can be about you personally or about human nature in general. Psychologists rarely ask this broader question, but we believe there are several common implicit beliefs about the nature of human "substance" (i.e., ontology) and what defines a person. Three main positions exist, though there are also shades in between.

1. Humans are physical beings whose bodies and actions are ultimately determined by the laws of physics. This view is sometimes called physicalism, and it is part of a larger philosophical view called monism (i.e., the view that there is only "one substance"; this contrasts with dualism, in which there are "two substances": body and mind). This position is often (but not always) accompanied by the ideas that—at our core—we are individuals (i.e., not deeply relational creatures) determined by biology and environment and that we ultimately have no agency (i.e., free will).

2. Humans are part of the natural world, but there is more to us than simply cause-and-effect events. Even though humans are made of material substance, and nothing more, we may have agency and be able to act willfully (i.e., without external causes). In other words, the mind cannot be reduced entirely to physical laws, and behavior is not determined by these laws. This view is often (but not always) accompanied by a view that we are "special" because of our relationships. To sum up, this position suggests that we are embodied but also embedded (i.e., defined by our relationships to other beings).

3. Humans are more than mere substance, so there must be some other element or substance added. The added element that makes humans special could be a nonmaterial mind, a soul, a spirit, or some combination of these elements. This view is often called dualism because it posits that there is at least one other part that makes a human being a thinking creature with agency and moral direction. This view may or may not be accompanied by a strong sense that we are defined by our relational nature.

For those in the first camp, all of existence can be reduced to simple cause-and-effect events. These events combine to create complex interactions and behaviors, but there is always an attempt to find the smallest elements that make up the larger actions (similar to identifying that water is made from molecules, which are made of atoms, which consist of protons, neutrons, and electrons). This idea, called reductionism, suggests that all behavior and mental phenomenon can be explained by social and physical events and biological factors (i.e., biological evolution, nerve cells, hormones, genetics).[1] These factors can theoretically be explained by chemistry, and all of chemistry ultimately follows the laws of physics. The logical outcome of this view is called determinism because it suggests that—once the world is set in motion—the laws of physics determine the next event and so on. Likewise, the mind is simply another way of describing the activity of the brain and is considered equal either to brain function (often called materialism[2]) or, for some, to an epiphenomenon. Calling consciousness an epiphenomenon is analogous to calling it lawn mower noise. A gas-powered lawn mower certainly makes noise—and the noise is very real—but the noise only tells you the machine is running; it does not impact the running of the machine. Consciousness and mental activity in general are considered by-products of the working brain. Conscious mental activity may be very real to the person producing the activity, but it does not impact behavior because the "machinery" of the brain has already made the decision. This of course leaves little or no room for agency.

This view is sometimes accompanied by a position that humans are ultimately individuals driven by survival motives. In his book *The Selfish Gene*, evolutionary biologist Richard Dawkins argues that our genetic material drives survival: "I shall argue that a predominant quality to be expected in a successful gene is ruthless selfishness. This gene selfishness will usually give rise to selfishness in individual behaviour. However, as we shall see, there are special circumstances in which a gene can achieve its own selfish goals best by fostering a limited form of altruism at the level of individual animals."[3] Therefore, while many organisms, including humans, can be helpful and demonstrate the im-

---

1. Leahey, *History of Modern Psychology*, 36.
2. Not to be confused with the desire for earthly possessions.
3. Quoted in Davis, *Analysis of Richard Dawkins's "The Selfish Gene,"* 3.

portance of relationships, the core tendency is toward self-preservation or individual survival.

The second view was not common until recent decades. However, a small but growing segment of philosophers, theologians, and secular *and* Christian psychologists has embraced this idea. The notion that we are entirely physical creatures and yet have free will is difficult to grasp—even for those proposing the idea—since it is hard to imagine a purely physical being that is not determined by physical forces. The common language used to describe this position uses two fancy terms: *emergent property* and *supervenience*.[4] Emergent property suggests that the mind emerges from the complex interaction of brain modules. In other words, the mind is greater than the sum of the parts on which it is built. The term *supervenience* comes from the idea that higher-order organization (i.e., "super" or "above") can influence lower-level properties. For example, the software of a computer (i.e., the higher-order organization) influences the electrons (i.e., lower-level physical actions) running through the computer. In the same way, a human mind (i.e., higher-level organization that emerges from brain activity) might drive the nerve cells and molecules on which that mind is based. (Yes, we know this gives you a headache when you think about it too long!) This view would also argue that without an embodied brain, mental activity ceases to exist.

This position is often accompanied by a view that humans are defined relationally. In other words, what makes a human being special if the concept of soul—the way we traditionally think of it—is not included? The answer from this group is that a person is special because of their relationships. Christian neuropsychologist Warren Brown describes the issue this way: "Thus, in this view, it is experiences of relatedness to others, to the self, and most particularly to God that endow a person with the attributes that have been attached to the concept of 'soul.' Experiences of personal relatedness, in their deepest and richest, create in us that which is semantically designated as 'soul.'"[5] In summary, this second position accepts the material nature

---

4. Murphy and Brown, *Did My Neurons Make Me Do It?*, 21.
5. Brown, "Cognitive Contributions to Soul," 102.

of human beings but rejects the idea that human thought and behavior are determined by this physical existence. In addition, we are special because we are in relationship to God, the world, and others.

The third position on human ontology has been the dominant view among the general population of the world and certainly among most Christians. This dual-substance idea appears, at least on the surface, to be not only compatible with many translations of Scripture but also consistent with ancient Greek philosophers such as Plato. During the Enlightenment, the philosopher René Descartes formalized this philosophy by proposing a special type of dualism called interactionism. In this view, the mind is a nonmaterial substance that interacts with the body but is apart from the body. The body has many built-in mechanisms, and it can influence the mind-soul, but in the end the mind-soul rules over the body. Many Christians in recent centuries have equated this mind with the idea of the soul and presume that the mind-soul is the seat of consciousness, creativity, moral decision making, and the will (i.e., the ability to act without external causes).

While these exemplars describe key positions, there are certainly other views that don't fit neatly within these categories. For example, theologian John Cooper has argued that in our current physical existence, we cannot speak of two things (i.e., body and soul) because we are unified, holistic, embodied creatures. However, at death God can extract from us that which constitutes our "essence." So only upon death can we talk about "two substances."[6]

In summarizing these positions, we can say that they place varying degrees of emphasis on our material or bodily existence. Even within the so-called dualistic position, there are varying degrees of emphasis on our material nature and the extent to which we are part of the natural world. Since this is such a complex issue, we have included a brief appendix that expands on these positions and provides additional clarity about their implications.

We believe that questions of ontology create strong, often unspoken assumptions that significantly impact how one understands the relationship between faith and psychology. If the mind is purely material

---

6. See Cooper, *Body, Soul, and Life Everlasting*.

and driven by selfish genes, then all mental activity can be reduced to deterministic influences and little room is left for discussions of agency, responsibility, or moral choices. If a psychologist believes that the mind-soul is something completely apart from the body and that this mind-soul is the seat of consciousness as well as of free will, then individuals with some form of brain-based mental disorder should be able to overcome such a disorder by sheer force of will. In addition, how can there be a "science of the mind" if the mind is not part of the physical world and therefore not open to scientific inquiry or prediction? If the mind is not predictable, then therapy should place greater emphasis on spiritual issues than on reasoning, emotions, or behavioral patterns. These are just some of the many issues in psychology impacted by this worldview question.

Where Am I Going? Issues of Agency, Purpose, and Meaning

There are essentially three major views when trying to understand agency, purpose, and meaning.

1. Natural and human history are based on the laws of physics, and all matter, all living creatures, and all human behavior are ultimately determined by cause-and-effect events. In this framework, the end goal (i.e., teleology) of humans may be seen as adaptation to and survival in the environment. Therefore, moral values (i.e., axiology) are dependent on what is valuable for survival. In this view, human free choice or agency is an illusion, and humans are responding to environmental forces rather than seeking meaning or working toward some larger goal.

2. The outcomes of history do not follow any pattern and are based on random events that cannot be predicted or known. This view is generally qualified by acknowledging that natural laws exist and that some aspects of reality and human behavior might be predictable, but over the course of time, none of this can be fully known. In addition, humans have true free will, so this potential variable means that human history cannot be predicted with

much certainty, except over very short periods of time. This view may or may not be accompanied by a view that stresses human meaning or goal seeking.

3. History follows a predetermined outcome that has been set by an all-knowing Creator. This view may be qualified by suggesting that there may be natural forces involved in the process and that human behavior may involve free choice, but the eventual outcomes (e.g., who is born, our character, significant social events) are either known in advance or predetermined in advance. This view is often accompanied by a view that stresses our desire for a deeper meaning or purpose.

These three positions capture a cross section of beliefs, but there is certainly a continuum of beliefs about causes, outcomes, and purposes. Those endorsing the first position, which, with some exceptions, was dominant in psychology during the first one hundred years of its history and perhaps still is today, tend to lean toward reductionism, determinism, and a rejection of human agency.[7] According to this view, the author's decision to switch jobs described at the beginning of the chapter was based on a whole sequence of events that ultimately resulted from physical forces. In theory, if we knew enough about all causes (i.e., external forces, past nerve cell responses), we could predict the behavioral outcome of any situation with 100 percent accuracy.

Not surprisingly, individuals who favor reductionism and determinism in psychology tend to approach social science research using strict positivism (i.e., facts about reality can be established with certainty) or perhaps a postpositivist approach. Th reductionist approach is associated with the view that the ultimate purpose or value of a thing can be determined only by its utility or value in promoting life or existence. Goodness is whatever helps us survive—not only as an individual but as a species. Humans are not seeking meaning or purpose but simply responding to biology and the environment.

The second view is associated with individuals who either are ambivalent about the nature of reality (i.e., agnostic) or place a high value

7. Bargh and Ferguson, "Beyond Behaviorism," 925.

on human freedom and responsibility. As described above, individuals may acknowledge some predictability for behavior, but random events and/or human volition (i.e., free choice or agency) make long-term predictions about human behavior difficult or impossible. Therefore, the best approach to studying social science is to understand the individual instead of discovering laws or long-term patterns that govern all behaviors. In this view, the author's decision to move his family was a combination of physical cause-and-effect events, random variations, and willful choices. Therefore, no one could have predicted (except for immediately before the event occurred) that the decision would be made. Individuals who favor this view also tend to favor either a constructivist view or a critical-ideological view for social science. Like the first view, there is no ultimate purpose or meaning to things or actions except for their utility in promoting life or a certain cultural or personal value. However, some who favor this view do believe that humans are meaning-seeking creatures (even though there is no ultimately correct meaning to find).

The third view concerning teleology and axiology is the one most religious people embrace. This approach does not necessarily deny cause-and-effect events but suggests that other factors impact the outcomes of our individual lives and human history in general. In addition, this view implies some form of value that is placed on outcomes. Some outcomes were designed as better (i.e., as God intended) than other outcomes. Some actions are inherently evil, while others are morally good. This is because of the value given to them at the beginning of time—even though they may also have temporal benefits (e.g., improving survivability, helping society function). For example, most Christian groups, as well as a variety of other religious traditions, propose that marriage involves a life-long monogamous commitment and that deviations from this (i.e., divorce, serial monogamy, adultery)—while unavoidable due to sin or the brokenness of society—were not the original intent or the desired outcome. They may argue further that marital relationships have societal benefit and may even help the survivability of offspring, but these are not the ultimate rationale for their existence. Finally, meaning and purpose can be defined as discovering and arriving at the correct outcome or intended goals. How do persons of faith attempt to relate the idea that there is a patterned and even lawful universe with the idea that God can work to accomplish his purposes? The answer is complex because diverse explanations, theological interpretations, and metaphors have been provided to give us some understanding. The simple and most honest answer is that we do not know, but in subsequent chapters, we will see how differing views might impact psychological science or applications.

In summarizing these positions, we can say that they place varying degrees of emphasis on human agency and on the larger purpose of existence. The teleological view one holds can have enormous impact on how one might approach psychology, but we provide just two illustrative examples here.

One good example comes from developmental psychology theories. Many developmental theories, such as those of Jean Piaget, Erik Erikson, and James Fowler, have an implicit teleological view.[8] In other words, they describe developmental changes that result in some good or bad outcome. But what determines a good or bad outcome? In some cases, goodness is defined in a utilitarian manner. For example, "Does the outcome allow the person to function better in their environment?" In other cases, it is established by a preexisting cultural or social view. For example, "Does the outcome produce greater individual autonomy and self-reliance?" Some Christian theories of development suggest that a good outcome is defined by preestablished biblical norms as to what kind of person each of us should be. For example, "Does the outcome reflect someone who is humble, slow to anger, and forgiving of others?" Any of these may be valid assumptions, but the key point is that they all reflect an extrascientific perspective as to what makes an outcome good.

Another example of teleology influencing psychology comes from the world of therapy. Therapists often differ on the best practices or processes in therapy, but they also differ on what constitutes a good outcome.[9] Is the goal of therapy to promote greater assertiveness and high self-esteem or to help someone see that others come first?

8. For a full discussion, see Moes and Tellinghuisen, *Exploring Psychology and Christian Faith*, 117–30.

9. McRay, Yarhouse, and Butman, *Modern Psychopathologies*, 95–105.

Of course, one's view of agency has implications for all aspects of psychology—from scientific descriptions of behavior to therapeutic interventions. If you feel that all behavior is determined by causal events, then you will likely approach scientific psychology using a strict positivist approach. If you feel that human agency is central to understanding people, then your therapy approach may focus much more on self-regulation and self-direction than on finding external constraints.

Am I Good or Bad? Issues of Moral Tendencies

The final key question related to anthropology involves basic moral tendencies. This includes but is not limited to questions about what constitutes a morally good choice (i.e., axiology). Again, there are three common positions on this question.

1. Humans are morally neutral. Human beings are not inherently prone toward evil or good but are simply survival machines trying to make their way through life as best they can.
2. Humans have a natural tendency toward being good (i.e., kind, just, helpful). While human beings may do bad things, the problem lies not within the basic nature of the person but in the situation, system, or context within which they exist.
3. Humans have a natural tendency toward evil. This position is often associated with many religious theologies but may overlap with some psychological theories, such as Freud's view of the id.

These basic views cut across psychological theories (as will be described in chap. 3), but they also vary among religious groups. Most Christian groups favor the latter view, but even within this view, the exact nature of evil and how it manifests itself are matters of some discussion and debate.[10] More on the latter point will be discussed in chapter 4 when we discuss theological worldviews, but at this point,

---

10. Gunnoe, *Person in Psychology and Christianity*, 20–32.

we can identify basic ways in which these views impact approaches to psychology.

Since the issue of sin or evil relates to personal behavior, much of the impact is felt in areas such as personality theory and counseling. Those who favor the first approach will simply look for causal events in biology or the environment to reduce "bad" behavior to more basic mechanisms. The second approach promotes attempts to find hinderances to becoming "all that we can be" in the environment but also within our own willful choices. The third approach may emphasize personal confession, personal accountability, or perhaps (in the case of psychoanalysis) uncovering deep, dark, destructive, and unconscious impulses. More on these applications will be discussed in subsequent chapters.

Faith Perspectives and Anthropology

What is notable about all the positions described in this chapter is that they represent extrascientific views. The positions a person selects will be heavily driven by their worldview rather than by data alone. Many scientists believe that the first position in each of these main areas (ontology, teleology, and axiology) is the only scientifically valid claim, but they would have to admit that there is no reasonable test for the hypothesis that could validate each claim.

In each of these main areas, the third position is viewed by many—but not all—as consistent with religious or specifically Christian views about human substance, purpose, and goodness. What you believe about these issues shapes your view concerning free will, responsibility, our basic substance, the goodness of humans, and the nature of human relationships. In chapter 3, we will see how these worldviews have shaped many schools of thought throughout the history of psychology. But what are some of those key biblical worldview positions concerning human nature that might influence one's approach to psychology?

One of the authors of this book (Paul Moes) and his colleague Don Tellinghuisen summarize what they believe to be some of the key biblical views of the person in their book *Exploring Psychology and Christian Faith*. They explain five themes about human nature that capture just some of the biblical narrative concerning our nature.

1. *Relational persons.* We are made in the image of God, and we are meant for relationship with him, others, and creation.
2. *Broken, in need of redemption.* We are sinners in need of salvation through Christ, living in and as part of a creation that suffers the consequences of all humanity's sin.
3. *Embodied.* We bear God's image in real bodies in a real world.
4. *Responsible limited agents.* We make choices (within constraints) that result in actions for which we are both individually and corporately responsible.
5. *Meaning seekers.* We seek to make sense of our surroundings, experiences, and purpose through our perception of patterns, through creative meaning making, and through a desire for a deity.[11]

Before we unpack these themes, just a word about their use. This list is not meant to be exhaustive, since additional aspects of human nature could be included. However, the list captures key elements that might be most relevant for relating faith to psychology. In addition, the list is not meant to dictate any specific approach when applying faith to psychology. Rather, the list provides one way to summarize the position of many Christians and, in fact, many religious people in general. We believe that most Christian psychologists[12] and even some secular psychologists[13] would find some or full agreement with many of these themes.

Let us examine a fuller description and application of each of these themes. First, being relational persons suggests that we have an ultimate purpose and a nature that go beyond our being individual response-generating machines. This theme does not ignore our physical nature or that we are embedded in a physical world, but it does imply that we have an innate tendency to be in relationship—with our Creator, the natural world, and one another. As Christian psychologists Brad

11. Moes and Tellinghuisen, *Exploring Psychology and Christian Faith*, ix.
12. For examples of similar themes, see Jeeves, *Human Nature at the Millennium*; Jones, *Psychology*; and McRay, Yarhouse, and Butman, *Modern Psychopathologies*.
13. For examples of relationality and meaning seeking in psychology, see Chomsky, *What Kind of Creatures Are We?*; and Lewin, *Dynamic Theory of Personality*.

Strawn and Warren Brown suggest, "Humans are relational beings. Most everything we experience from conception to death includes others to some degree. We experience, learn, think, create, and imagine as bodies who are embedded in relational networks. The truth of the matter is that we are never truly alone. Even when we are absorbed in silent thought, we are mostly engaging in imaginary relations with others from our past, present, or an anticipated future."[14]

Being broken and in need of redemption implies several things about human nature. First, we were created good, meaning that we had a natural inclination to seek after what is good (i.e., as God designed it). However, with the curse of sin, our nature has been tainted or corrupted (depending on your theological viewpoint). In addition, both the natural order and the social order have been damaged as the result of individual actions, but they have also become distorted at a system level. So, we have disease, death, social inequities, and so on that are not the result the actions of one individual but the result of how the system does not work. In chapter 4 we will examine subtle differences among Christians concerning the nature of sin. We will show in chapter 3 how various schools of thought in psychology appear to stress that humans are prone toward self-serving or selfish ends, are prone toward more noble or positive ends, or are essentially neutral in nature—simply trying to maximize the most optimal survival benefits.

As described earlier in this chapter, our embodied existence is an important theme in much of Scripture. This is a theme that many secular psychologists have stressed but that is often ignored by many Christians. Whatever view one takes concerning the existence of an ethereal (i.e., nonmaterial) soul, many biblical scholars believe that Scripture regularly emphasizes our bodily existence.[15]

Being responsible limited agents emphasizes three aspects of human nature and human behavior. First, we bear responsibility for actions that were freely chosen. We also, to some extent, bear responsibility for those actions that may have been done "mindlessly" or as part of

14. Strawn and Brown, *Enhancing Christian Life*, 116–17.
15. Hall, "What Are Bodies For?," 159.

collective action. Being agents implies that we do have the capacity to direct our actions without external cause. Finally, being limited suggests that despite our responsibilities and our agency, we also have many constraints that limit our free choices. While not yielding to strict determinism, we do acknowledge that genetic, biological, habitual, and social constraints affect our choices and behavior. A small number of secular psychologists express similar sentiments by suggesting that even if a great deal of our behavior is driven by "natural forces," this does not rule out the possibility of "agency."[16] In other words, we are *limited* agents.

Finally, being meaning seekers implies that we are more than response-generating machines. We do not just respond to rewards and punishments, or make simple associations, or even passively create cognitive schemas. Instead, we actively seek information, attempt to make sense of it, and attempt to fit it into a broader understanding of the world. This relates to small questions (e.g., Why does that light switch work that way?) as well as to large questions (e.g., Why am I here? How was I made?).

We will return to these themes in later chapters, but for now you might be able to see that viewing humans as responsible yet limited agents and as broken but relational meaning seekers *could* potentially shape your view of psychological theories and even research findings. The question raised by several Christian psychologists is whether they *should* influence our science and practice or perhaps whether they should dominate our psychology over and against basic science findings. These questions will be addressed in chapters 5–8.

QUESTIONS FOR DISCUSSION

1. Think about your own personal history or religious beliefs. How do you view issues such as sin, free will, and embodiment?

2. Despite all the worldview issues raised in this chapter, would it be better for the field of psychology to try to avoid discussion

16. Nahmias, "Why We Have Free Will."

of these complex issues and just stick to describing behavior as objectively as possible? Explain.

3. Do you feel that the Christian church has emphasized the strong limitations on our free will, or has it emphasized *unlimited* agency? What implications are there for psychology when adopting either extreme?

3

Views in Contemporary Psychology

The greatest discovery of my generation is that human beings can alter their lives by altering their attitudes of mind.

William James, quoted in Joseph A. Smith's *Love's Mystery Solved*

The disappearance of a sense of responsibility is the most far-reaching consequence of submission to authority.

Stanley Milgram, "The Dilemma of Obedience"

The two quotations above reflect perspectives that have not been common among psychologists. William James, the first significant American psychologist, believed that people can willfully change their thoughts and behavior, and the well-known social psychologist Stanley Milgram suggested that people should feel a sense of responsibility for their actions. As we will see in this chapter, psychology has been dominated by worldviews that reflect reductionistic, positivistic, and deterministic positions (see chaps. 1 and 2 for full descriptions)—although we will also describe a weakening of this dominance. If taken to their logical conclusion, these positions leave little or no room for free will or responsibility. Despite the desire by some for psychology to be a purely objective science that is uninfluenced by worldviews, extrascientific concepts have influenced theories and practices throughout the history of psychology (as well as many other scientific disciplines). These concepts are extrascientific because they cannot be fully confirmed or falsified by data. Some ideas come in the form of narrow theories that summarize patterns found in studies, but others address larger questions of ontology, teleology, and axiology. In addition, these extrascientific views have varied a great deal across several schools of thought as well as various subdisciplines (e.g., clinical, social, developmental) within the field.

Why is this topic important to explore? Because various nonscientific worldviews that have shaped the discipline can impact how one integrates faith with psychology. For example, if a Christian is trying to relate faith to psychology and says, "I cannot relate my faith to psychology because of its deterministic viewpoint," they should understand that not all schools of thought adhere to a deterministic view (even though many do). Likewise, someone of faith may object to perspectives that point to our very "dark" nature, or perhaps our generally noble character, or perhaps our generally neutral moral tendency. But as with determinism, more than one perspective about human nature is reflected in the field, so no one can criticize all of psychology based on a single issue. In addition, the field of psychology has evolved over the years, so it is important to see how faith may relate to contemporary issues. Showing that a long-abandoned approach to psychology is incompatible with elements of Christian faith, as some have done, is useful only in historical context—it does little to help us understand integration in the present. In summary, to relate faith to psychology, we need to understand the subfield, the time period, and the "brand" of psychology we are discussing.

In the rest of this chapter, we present a brief historical overview of psychological views. In each case we examine how the approach aligns with the themes of human nature described in chapter 2 to see how it may or may not be easily integrated with Christian perspectives. Why compare these schools of thought with the themes of human nature?

The primary point is not to show that a given approach is correct or incorrect, nor is it to promote one model of integration over another (see chaps. 5–8). It is to emphasize that many of the assumptions of each school reflect extrascientific views. Certainly, there are areas of psychology where worldview issues have less apparent impact (e.g., neurotransmitter differences associated with depression), but in other areas the influence could potentially be significant (e.g., personality theories concerning human goodness).

Functionalism

Functionalism is one of the lesser-known schools of thought in the history of psychology. The principal ideas forming this approach were generated by the late nineteenth-century American psychologist William James.[1] James and others believed that conscious processes should be the focus of psychological study and that actions must be functional (i.e., useful) in promoting survival. While evolution shapes our biological traits, he believed that evolution also gave us mental and behavioral mechanisms for learning and adapting to changing environments. Therefore, while humans are governed by many instinctual behaviors and habits, we also have the capacity to change our behavior and to act "willfully." Functionalism was criticized by others as being too "mental," not empirical enough, too ill-defined, and too practical (but for others not practical enough); as a result, it did not continue as a cohesive school of thought for very long. Rather than disappear entirely, the approach morphed into other schools of thought, such as behaviorism and later cognitive-behavioral approaches.[2]

While functionalism is long gone from the scene, we mention it because it foreshadows several contemporary ideas about mental activity and behavior. Contemporary psychology adheres more rigorously to empirical observation, but many of the ideas that stress conscious thought and even the possibility of willful mental activity are once again considered acceptable ideas, or at least reasonable possibilities.

1. See James, *Psychology.*
2. C. Green, "Darwinian Theory."

In addition, the functional nature of behavior in adapting to changing situations is increasingly stressed in evolutionary psychology.

James believed in pragmatism, which suggests that truth is determined based on coherence of thought as well as the practical value of any prediction.[3] This approach appears to approximate a more postpositivist approach, which is consistent with the fact that he and others in this movement were very willing to theorize about mental processes even though they could not directly observe these qualities. In other words, it was acceptable to apply reason and inference when examining data and to realize that "the world conceived" was not the same as "the world perceived."[4]

In terms of their view of human nature, functionalists saw humans not as inherently good or inherently evil but as neutral; our character comes about from our experiences and the choices we make. They also stressed our relational nature, our embodied nature, and our meaning-seeking tendency. Finally, the approach stressed that, despite limitations and constraints, we have the capacity to be willful and responsible creatures.[5] Therefore, this approach would not be considered particularly deterministic or reductionistic in nature. Several of these functionalist ideas appear to be compatible with the biblical themes described in chapter 2. This is important to note since, as mentioned earlier, not all schools of thought in psychology completely contradict biblical views of human nature, as some have contended.

Psychoanalytic and Psychodynamic Approaches

Psychoanalysis owes much of its existence to Sigmund Freud. Most students will be aware of the beginnings of psychoanalytic thought and its more contemporary "cousin" the psychodynamic approach, so we are providing only a cursory overview of the approach here. Freud, like James, was heavily influenced by Charles Darwin and his theory of evolution.[6] However, Freud applied the ideas in a very different way.

3. See James, *Pragmatism and Four Essays*.
4. James, *Will to Believe*, 118.
5. James, *Will to Believe*, 146.
6. See Sulloway, *Freud*.

Freud believed that the unconscious mind, which is a reservoir of our inherited animal instincts, determines most of our everyday behaviors. Two instincts that he considered most important for survival are sex drives (to propagate the species) and aggression (for survival of the fittest). These drives are largely confined to that portion of our unconscious mind called the id. The largely conscious ego evolved to resolve the conflicts that arise from our ancient id clashing with the rules of culture as well as our semiconscious superego, which provides a moral compass. While the ego and the superego are important elements of the mind, the id ultimately "drives the system" so to speak. In the end, the other two components are always wrestling with the unconscious drives that emanate from the id.[7] The therapeutic approach involved exploring and interpreting dreams as well as hidden impulses (i.e., Freudian slips) and allowing these unconscious impulses to be brought into consciousness.

It is difficult to characterize Freud's epistemology. He viewed himself as practicing an empirical positivist science, but given his propensity to base theories on very limited observations, critics have argued that he used a constructivist approach.[8] The approach was strongly criticized by many individuals over the years for being unscientific and lacking verifiable predictions,[9] for its emphasis on sexuality and aggression as the primary motivations,[10] and for its rather dark view of human nature—to mention only a few key issues.

How does psychoanalysis compare to the five themes of human nature described in chapter 2? Freud's approach can be considered deterministic in that our behavior is determined largely by forces outside our conscious control. Even when we believe that we are directing our own behavior by way of the ego, the ego is simply responding to the social rules and unconscious drives in the simplest possible way. Therefore, Freud would have downplayed our being responsible agents and would have emphasized our limited nature. He also viewed humans as basically self-serving and even selfish at their core. Because we are driven

7. N. Smith, *Current Systems in Psychology*, 146–47.
8. Robinson and Robinson, *Freud and His Critics*, 261.
9. See Seligman et al., "Navigating into the Future."
10. Robinson and Robinson, *Freud and His Critics*, 90.

by basic survival instincts, our core motivation is self-preservation—
even at the expense of others. Therefore, one could argue that people
are broken in this view, but because Freud believed that a person can
manage their impulses but not change their fundamental character,
full redemption (i.e., restoration of a relationship with God) is not
possible in his scheme.

Historic psychoanalytic thought was also relatively individualistic. While there was considerable stress on the nature of parent-child
relationships, psychoanalytic therapy focused on probing the unconscious mind as the method of treatment, so there was little emphasis on
our relational nature in determining change. The approach did stress
embodiment to some extent in that the mind is fully an outgrowth of
our biological substance, but Freud also believed that some physical
conditions (e.g., loss of feeling in a hand) could be the result of mental
processes (e.g., repressed anxiety). Therefore, the mind has properties that cannot be reduced to neurological states alone and in fact can
alter bodily function. It is difficult to determine whether Freud and
others felt that we are meaning-seeking creatures. He did emphasize
our tendency to explain (i.e., rationalize) our thoughts and behaviors,
but this form of meaning seeking was almost always distorted and
ultimately irrational.

Psychodynamic thought, which is a more common and contemporary outgrowth of psychoanalysis, has changed many of the foundational views of Freud and his early followers. The emphasis on sexual
and aggressive urges; the "psychic conflict" created by the id, ego, and
superego; the rather "dark" (i.e., self-serving) view of human nature;
the strong determinism of the unconscious mind; and the absence of
empirical and replicable studies have all been softened or eliminated
from contemporary approaches.[11] For example, individuals with a psychodynamic orientation are much more open to independent verifi-
cation of observations and doing larger outcome studies to verify the
legitimacy of various theories and practices. Despite that, it is safe to
say that the research paradigm would clearly lean toward constructivist
approaches. What has remained relatively constant is an adherence to

11. N. Smith, *Current Systems in Psychology*, 148–71.

a more individualistic approach in therapy as well as a strong emphasis on unconscious processes determining much (but perhaps not all) of our behavior.

Behaviorism

More will be said about the nature and history of behaviorism in chapter 5, but we provide an outline of this approach here. The early twentieth-century American psychologist John Watson is often considered the father of this school of thought.[12] Watson believed that psychology should only focus on what can be observed or directly controlled. Watson carried forward ideas from Ivan Pavlov and E. L. Thorndike, who had both demonstrated previously that one could carefully manipulate variables in the environment and determine a behavioral outcome. Watson confidently declared, "Give me a dozen healthy infants, well-formed, and my own specified world to bring them up in and I'll guarantee to take any one at random and train him to become any type of specialist I might select—doctor, lawyer, artist, merchant-chief and, yes, even beggar-man and thief, regardless of his talents, penchants, tendencies, abilities, vocations, and race of his ancestors."[13]

Famous for his demonstrations of fear conditioning using the small child referred to as "little Albert," Watson was able to show that simply by manipulating observable variables (i.e., a loud noise accompanied by the presentation of a small animal), he could create a child with a specific fear.[14] Watson ridiculed the speculative nature of Freud's approach by stating,

> The Freudians twenty years from now, . . . when they come to analyze Albert's fear of a seal skin coat . . . will probably tease from him a recital of a dream which upon their analysis will show that Albert at three years of age attempted to play with the pubic hair of the mother and was scolded violently for it. If the analyst has sufficiently prepared

12. Hilgard, *Psychology in America*, 88–91.
13. J. Watson, *Behaviorism*, 82.
14. Schultz and Schultz, *History of Modern Psychology*, 292–93.

Albert to accept such a dream, . . . he may be fully convinced that the dream was a true revealer of the factors which brought about the fear.[15]

In the mid-twentieth century, B. F. Skinner carried the mantle of behaviorism and brought the philosophical implications to their logical conclusions. Like Watson, he was confident that learned behaviors (as opposed to genetic or endowed traits) are the basis of human tendencies, that learned behaviors can be manipulated to create any desired outcome, and that all behaviors are ultimately determined by conditions in the environment (i.e., rewards and punishments). He rejected any suggestion that one can attribute behavior to internal causes. Skinner wrote that free will is a myth and believed that through the principles of behaviorism, society can achieve a near utopian-like existence.[16] Skinner wrote in 1978—just as a cognitive revolution was taking place in psychology—that "we need to change our behavior and we can do so only by changing our physical and social environments. We choose the wrong path at the very start when we suppose that our goal is to change the 'minds and hearts of men and women' rather than the world in which they live."[17] Behaviorism, along with the basic tools of classical and operant conditioning, was the dominant paradigm in psychology for several decades, and it led to many educational and clinical applications, such as applied behavior analysis.[18]

As is evident from this brief overview, behaviorism has a very strong positivist, reductionist, and deterministic perspective. Only through direct observation can one obtain indisputable factual truth. All behavior change can be reduced to simple associations and consequences that somehow become connected or programmed. Conscious mental activity is dismissed as an epiphenomenon (like lawn mower noise—see chap. 2) of brain activity and has little relevance for understanding behavior.

Comparing the five themes of human nature to behaviorist views reveals starkly contrasting worldviews. Humans are viewed as neutral

15. Watson and Rayner, "Conditioned Emotional Reactions," 12–14.
16. See Skinner, *Walden Two*.
17. Skinner, "Why I Am Not a Cognitive Psychologist," 10.
18. Applied behavior analysis (ABA) employs behavioral observation along with many operant conditioning principles—in addition to a variety of other behavioral techniques—to promote change.

creatures (i.e., neither inherently good nor inherently evil), with our characteristics formed entirely by environmental factors (i.e., as opposed to genetics, the unconscious mind, or willful decisions). The only "brokenness" is the brokenness of society, which uses incorrect methods to change behaviors (i.e., too much punishment or incorrect rewards). Behaviorists do not speak of relationality as a profound and deeply meaningful bond. Instead, they reduce relationships to transactional interactions in that one person provides consequences for the behavior of another and vice versa. There is no room for a discussion of agency because we are completely limited by environmental constraints. Humans are not meaning-seeking creatures. We do not actively shape or interpret our experiences. Instead, we are passive responders to stimuli and consequences. Behaviorists did stress embodiment to some degree in that the learned associations that we experience were presumed to exist somewhere or somehow in the nervous system. However, Skinner downplayed genetic or biological explanations for behavior, so despite his mechanistic outlook, our embodied existence is a minor element of this approach.

Humanistic Psychology

Abraham Maslow is credited with promoting most of the foundational ideas that formed the humanistic approach. This mid-twentieth-century movement was a reaction to the unconscious determinism of Freud and the environmental determinism of behaviorism. Maslow felt that humans can direct their own futures and that they must take responsibility for their actions. He also believed that people are capable of self-improvement. If given the right opportunities and tools, people can and will inevitably reach their full potential (i.e., self-actualization) and become motivated by purely noble goals. Carl Rogers extended and applied many of Maslow's ideas to what he called client-centered therapy.[19] This is a nondirective approach to therapy in which the therapist simply guides the client toward self-understanding.

19. See Rogers, *Client-Centered Therapy*.

Maslow adhered to a constructivist approach to social science investigation and avoided any talk of scientific reductionism found in most other perspectives. Maslow famously wrote, "If the study of the uniqueness of the individual does not fit into what we know of science, then so much the worse for that conception of science. It, too, will have to endure re-creation."[20]

Rogers did promote regular investigations of therapy outcomes, but the approach rarely involved careful control or manipulation of variables. For these reasons, psychologists leaning toward a more behavioral or cognitive approach have felt that the humanistic approach lacks the type of scientific rigor needed in psychology. Some non-Western and feminist critics of humanistic psychology have suggested that the concept of self-actualization (i.e., be all that you can be) possesses a masculine[21] and cultural[22] bias. Despite these concerns, humanistic psychology has remained an important thread in the evolution of the field and has morphed into other movements, such as positive psychology, which stresses human potential and flourishing over psychological disturbances.[23]

The five themes of human nature align reasonably well with some of the key tenets of humanistic psychology. It, more than the other approaches, stresses humans as responsible limited agents. It also places a great deal of emphasis on meaning seeking. However, while not ignoring embodiment, humanistic psychology does not emphasize it. Maslow did stress our relational nature since he believed that authentic lives are lived in harmony with others. On the other hand, the concept of self-actualization is individualistic since one's inner potential may or may not be impacted by any social or cultural influence. So the primary teleology (i.e., goal or purpose) is not relational. One area in which humanistic psychology most definitely does not align with the five themes of human nature is the notion of being broken. Humanistic psychologists recognize social ills and constraints, but all people have the capacity within them to become a better or even perfect person.

20. Maslow, *Toward a Psychology of Being*, 10.
21. See Cullen, "Feminism, Management, and Self-Actualization."
22. See Ebersole and DeVore, "Self-Actualization, Diversity, and Meaning in Life," 37.
23. Rennie, "Two Thoughts on Abraham Maslow."

Cognitive Perspectives

Contemporary psychology is dominated by a cognitive or cognitive-behavioral perspective. This perspective traces its beginnings to the early days of psychology. Elements from William James and functionalism, the lesser-known Gestalt psychology, and the writings of Edward Tolman in the 1930s all contributed to concepts used today.[24] However, Jean Piaget, the well-known developmental psychologist, is often cited as a key figure in developing the basic concepts of this perspective.[25] What distinguishes this approach from behaviorism is an emphasis on mental operations as key to understanding behavior. Behaviorists saw mental operations as unobservable and therefore not worthy of study. Those following the cognitive approach are willing to infer these operations based on observable behaviors. In addition, they believe that humans have the capacity to use reason and to organize incoming information using a top-down process—in other words, we use preexisting knowledge structures to select, interpret, or shape incoming information. This stands in contrast to the more passive form of learning and behavior change that occurs with the behaviorist approach. The cognitive perspective dominates many subfields, including developmental psychology, social psychology, therapy, and portions of neuropsychology. Some have criticized the cognitive approach as being too "sterile" because of its lack of emphasis on emotions and other more dynamic aspects of mental functioning (e.g., motivation, unconscious processes).[26] However, in recent years, greater attention has been given to these issues.

Like behaviorists, cognitive psychologists use carefully controlled experiments to understand human thinking and behavior, so most would prefer a positivist or postpositivist research approach. When carried to its logical conclusions, the cognitive approach is considered reductionistic and deterministic. Most cognitive psychologists would assume that they can predict a person's next action if they have sufficient detail about that person's past and present experiences. In other words,

24. Seligman et al., "Navigating into the Future," 123.
25. Schultz and Schultz, *History of Modern Psychology*, 469.
26. Schultz and Schultz, *History of Modern Psychology*, 483.

even though we do not respond passively to our current circumstances, past situations have shaped our thought structures so that we are ultimately determined by past events. Despite this prevailing assumption, this reductionistic and deterministic perspective is emphasized less by proponents of the approach. In addition, as we will describe shortly, some cognitively oriented psychologists have recently allowed for the possibility of human agency.

The cognitive approach is very similar to the behaviorist approach in the way they understand human nature. For example, cognitive psychologists would view human nature as neutral (i.e., neither good nor bad) and would place only slightly greater emphasis on humans being embodied, relational, and responsible (i.e., possibly having agency). However, the greatest difference from a behaviorist approach is that cognitive psychologists allow more room for seeing humans as meaning-seeking creatures, since they stress the development of mental schemas that influence perception.

Behavioral Neuroscience and Evolutionary Psychology

In addition to cognitive perspectives on behavior, contemporary psychological thinking is increasingly dominated by neuroscience and evolutionary psychology. Neuroscience directs attention to our embodied existence by showing the profound ways that our behavior is influenced by genetics and brain function. Evolutionary psychology posits that natural selection selects not just for biological traits but also for behavioral traits and that many—if not most—of our behavioral tendencies develop this way. Both areas have been extremely helpful in providing evidence and theories about the purpose of some behaviors. As William James had foreshadowed in the early days of psychology, behaviors must have a function or a purpose or else they would not persist. While providing very helpful insights, these areas have also led some within the field to move toward a more reductionistic and deterministic framework that goes beyond what behaviorism was promoting. From this perspective, some have suggested that virtually all behaviors can be reduced to biological and genetic events that have roots in our evolutionary past. This view clearly favors a very positivist approach to science.

Despite the strong positivist, reductionist, and determinist impulses behind much of behavioral neuroscience, some voices have suggested that humans may still have agency or free will, even within a "closed" neurological system. In addition, research in both evolutionary psychology and neuroscience has supported the notion that humans are inherently relational creatures because species that are able to form complex and intimate social bonds are more likely to survive. Finally, several cognitive neuroscientists and evolutionary psychologists have stressed the importance of meaning seeking as a significant aspect of human life. They suggest that this explains many human tendencies, such as our desire to explore the natural world and even our desire to have religious explanations for existence.

As a result of these shifting ideas, it can be difficult to evaluate how these areas of psychology compare to the five themes of human nature. For some individuals within this group, humans are not responsible agents but only limited or determined; others in the group leave room for agency. Some suggest that humans are defined individually and are response-generating machines, while others view people as relational and meaning-seeking creatures. Certainly, all individuals in this group would emphasize our embodiment to some degree, and most would consider human nature to be morally neutral.

Subfields and Current Trends

As the field of psychology has matured, it has become increasingly specialized, with distinct perspectives dominating in each subfield. Fields such as developmental psychology, social psychology, personality psychology, psychopathology, gender studies, cognitive psychology, behavioral neuroscience, clinical assessment, and therapy all carry different sets of issues and perspectives and even research methods. In addition, the discipline continues to evolve and change with even greater rapidity as the number of researchers and clinicians grows and new discoveries are made. As described previously, even areas that were thought to lean heavily toward a positivist and reductionist view have been softened by some leading figures as they speculate about agency, relationality, and meaning-seeking tendencies. For example, leading social psychologists such as Martin Seligman, Roy Baumeister, and colleagues have proposed that humans use "prospection" (i.e., thinking about future events), which for these authors is a form of willful decision making.[27]

The diverse and ever-changing landscape of the field makes relating faith to psychology a difficult task. It also implies that many approaches that will be discussed in subsequent chapters may be relevant for some areas (e.g., therapy) but less useful in others (e.g., cognitive neuroscience). In addition, a concern about a particular worldview dominant in the field may not be relevant a few years later as that worldview shifts or becomes less prevalent. For example, some Christian psychologists have rightfully identified concepts from psychoanalytic thought that are difficult to square with a Christian worldview only to witness the general diminishment of psychoanalytic thought within the field—thus making the issues of integration in relation to that movement a moot point.

Therefore, while we will not promote a single approach to the integration of faith and psychology as the correct approach, we will identify problems with some approaches due to their being outdated and not incorporating current worldview questions. For readers trying to determine which approach seems most personally compatible and useful, it will be important to realize that approaches to integration can never be static but must constantly be updated and revised as the field changes and as our understanding of human behavior changes.

QUESTIONS FOR DISCUSSION

1. Which psychological school of thought seems most compatible with your view of psychology and why?
2. Would it be better for psychology if there was more effort to just describe and summarize the data from observations and to avoid the inclusion of worldview perspectives by way of these schools of thought? Is that even possible? Explain.

27. See Seligman et al., "Navigating into the Future."

3. Should Christians develop a distinct school of thought, separate from those presented in this chapter? Would it be better to adopt the perspective that appears most compatible with Christian faith or to refine one of the more compatible approaches?

4

Views in Contemporary Religion

Science can purify religion from error and superstition. Religion can purify science from idolatry and false absolutes.

Pope John Paul II, Letter to the Reverend George V. Coyne, SJ

For most of American history, of course, the important religious divides were between denominations—not just between Protestants and Catholics and Jews but between Lutherans and Episcopalians and Southern Baptists and the other endlessly fine-tuned sects.

Hanna Rosin, "Beyond Belief"

An old joke tells about a man being rescued from a tiny desert island after being alone for some time. The ship's captain asks the man about the three huts on the island. The man replies that the first hut is where he lived, and the second hut is his church. "What was the purpose of the third hut?" asks the captain. "Oh," the man replies, "that's the church I used to go to."

As the joke implies, there is a lot of disunity within the Christian church. In fact, "church unity" sounds like an oxymoron in the splintered landscape of the Christian church. And when we add other world religions to the mix, it is easy to be disillusioned about the nature of religious truth when there are so many "truths" from which to pick. In this chapter, we will explore a small sample of key differences among Christian groups. Why address these differences in a book about relating faith to psychology? Because a person's religious beliefs impact the way they view knowledge, science, human nature, and the wider society or culture—which in turn influences their view of psychology. Do you feel that academic learning is neutral and distinct from spiritual matters? Do you feel that Christians should be actively engaged in social, cultural, or political activities or that they should stay away from such activities? What is the nature of sin, and how might this relate to psychological issues? Should psychology become more of an exploration of the soul as opposed to a science of human behavior? The answers to these and many related questions can have a profound impact on your view of psychology.

Because exploring all world religions is beyond the scope of this book, we will focus on differences within the Christian church, but one could easily find similar strains in other world religions. We cannot describe the vast landscape of Christian teachings within a single chapter. Rather, we hope to identify key teachings or perspectives that are most directly related to how one understands science, knowledge, the wider society, and the nature of the person.

We must point out that the descriptions we provide here are based on broad generalizations. Individuals within various traditions or church groups may or may not adhere to all the teachings or perspectives of a group. You may find yourself saying, "I belong to that church group or denomination, but I don't think or feel that way!" In addition, while we describe positions as static, keep in mind that many views rest somewhere on a continuum rather than in categories or at extremes. However, there are certain teachings that *may* impact the way many people apply their faith in the world; some of these teachings may be implicit or unspoken, while others are part of formal church doctrine.

Many foundational issues divide Christian groups, such as views concerning biblical inerrancy, the role of the Holy Spirit, history and the future (e.g., dispensational views about future time periods and the second coming of Christ), and even church governance. While any of these issues can influence how one approaches psychology, we believe that views concerning nature and grace and views regarding the person have the largest impact on the approach one takes toward society, science, and psychology in particular.

Nature and Grace

In a religious context, *nature* refers to the entire physical world that we can observe. *Grace* can have several connotations but typically refers to God's actions toward the world we know. This action includes salvation issues (i.e., God's forgiveness of sin) but commonly refers more broadly to all the ways that God interacts with the natural world—including humans. The Dutch theologian Herman Bavinck poses the issue of nature and grace this way: "How is grace related to nature? . . . What is the connection between creation and re-creation, of the rich of the earth and the kingdom of heaven, of humanity and Christianity, of that which is below and that which is above?"[1] He goes on to stress the importance of this issue by stating, "Every Christian must take into account two factors: creation and re-creation, nature and grace, earthly and heavenly vocation, etc.; and in accordance with the different relationship in which he puts these to each other, his religious life assumes a different character."[2]

How does God view the natural world, and how should Christians interact or engage with that world? Bavinck suggests that the answer has a profound impact on a believer's religious and civic lives. We believe this is certainly the case. Whether or not we are aware of what our particular "brand" of religion teaches about nature and grace, we are convinced that these ideas influence us in profound ways. So let's examine a small sample of views about these concepts.

Nature-and-Grace Dualism

The term *dualism* in this context suggests that the natural world is very much apart from the spiritual or heavenly world and that these

1. Veenhof, "Nature and Grace in Bavinck," 3. "Rich" here refers to riches or to the richness of the earth.
2. Veenhof, "Nature and Grace in Bavinck," 3.

two worlds cannot be unified into one—at least not in current existence. Some church historians trace this thinking back to the medieval church figure Thomas Aquinas, though others have suggested that this is a misrepresentation of Thomistic thinking.[3] Aquinas's view is often characterized as "grace perfects nature."[4] In this view, the natural world is not evil, but it is also not sacred or sanctified. Only by God's grace, working through redeemed humans, can there be an elevation of nature. However, since nature is not part of the supernatural or divine world, it is always of lesser value and does not reach the same status as the sacred.

Some church leaders took these ideas to mean that the study of the natural world was relatively neutral and could be examined according to natural law apart from religious ideas. Natural law, according to Robert Cochran, is "the notion that reason provides a means of understanding which morals and laws lead to the highest level of human welfare."[5] In other words, just and fair laws can be understood as being built into the fabric of nature. Nature is understandable using human reason, while spiritual truth is grounded in revelation. Truth seeking grounded in reason—while aided by grace—is still inherent in all humans (i.e., part of our nature) and can be accomplished even by the "unredeemed" person if sufficient natural reason is applied. In one version of this view, human reasoning may not be perfect, but it is relatively unaffected by sin or by the "brokenness" of the world.[6] Therefore, this approach separates many academic pursuits (e.g., inductive and deductive reasoning, scientific conclusions) from religious understanding, since religious understanding is not seen as necessary for the process. Religious understanding is applied to only spiritual or moral issues. This tendency is seen in many colleges and universities that have a religious affiliation (i.e., are supported by a church body)

---

3. Cooper, "Body-Soul Question," 9.

4. Leibniz, "Principles of Nature and of Grace," 5.

5. Cochran, *Faith and Law*, 175.

6. For some Protestant scholars, this simply means that all people have the *potential* to find truth but that reason, unaided by the special grace of God, is unreliable at best. For others, natural law implies that reason is unaffected by sin and can therefore lead to truth even for those who are "unredeemed." For a full discussion, see Cochran, *Faith and Law*.

but try to maintain a more neutral stance when exploring nature. For some, particularly within the Roman Catholic tradition, this idea led to an attempt to transcend or be apart from the natural world and to pursue the spiritual. Monastic traditions that stressed personal piety, spiritual meditation, and being set apart from the rest of society were, in part, an outgrowth of this separation of nature and grace.

Again, this view elevates the sacred and the spiritual and tends to downplay or possibly even denigrate the "mundane" physical aspects of life. It does not condemn everyday activities that involve the physical world, but it does view them as temporal or lesser pursuits. Some theologians in the contemporary Roman Catholic Church have modified some of this dualism and have stressed the need for a more unified understanding of nature and grace.[7]

Two-kingdoms theory. A concept related to nature-and-grace dualism is the two-kingdoms theory. This view is often attributed to the church reformer Martin Luther, or at least to some of his followers,[8] and is still a theme in many Lutheran colleges and universities. Theologian John Witte Jr. summarizes the theory this way:

> The earthly kingdom is distorted by sin and governed by the Law. The Heavenly kingdom is renewed by grace and guided by the Gospel. A Christian is a citizen of both kingdoms at once and invariably comes under the distinctive government of each. As a heavenly citizen, the Christian remains free in his or her conscience, called to live fully by the light of the Word of God. But as an earthly citizen, the Christian is bound by law, and called to obey the natural orders and offices that God has ordained and maintained for the Governments of this earthly kingdom.[9]

In other words, there are two separate realms. People of faith live in both worlds simultaneously, but in this scheme the activities of their daily lives—what some might call their "secular pursuits"—are simply to be carried out according to the rules set by society or the rules of science. While a Christian is still responsible to live according to the

---

7. Curran, *Catholic Social Teaching*, 53.
8. Carson, *Christ and Culture Revisited*, 210–12.
9. Witte, *Law and Protestantism*, 5.

laws of the heavenly kingdom, they must also respect the laws of the earthly kingdom. Only when there is direct conflict in the case of moral or ethical issues is there a true tension between the two worlds.

Niebuhr's relation of Christ and culture. Another way to think about nature-and-grace dualism is through the writings of theologian H. Richard Niebuhr. Niebuhr outlines five approaches that Christians have historically taken toward culture, which includes social rules, government, cultural activities (e.g., art, literature, designing cities), and even science. These approaches are (1) Christ against culture, (2) Christ of culture, (3) Christ above culture, (4) Christ and culture in paradox, and (5) Christ the transformer of culture.[10] In each approach "Christ" is used as a stand-in for "church." While Donald Carson rightly suggests that many of these views require some updating within contemporary thought, they still serve as a useful heuristic in identifying common patterns. We will discuss the first and last of these views a bit later, but here we will focus on the middle three approaches because they provide some additional nuance (i.e., subtypes) for the notion of nature-and-grace dualism.

The Christ-of-culture approach accepts that there are two worlds—the natural and the sacred—but since both worlds are under the lordship of Christ, Christians should feel free to engage in many cultural activities. In this view, there is no need to elevate or perfect (as was suggested by Aquinas) the natural world, social movements, or cultural activities, since they have intrinsic value. Only those aspects of science, society, or the wider culture that are in direct conflict with Christian religion (which proponents of this view suggest is rare) need to be filtered out. Niebuhr characterizes this group as practicing a more progressive or liberal form of religion in that these individuals are much more comfortable engaging with the broader society. Therefore, this approach is somewhat less dualistic. It sees culture and Christ as separate but also relatively harmonious.

The Christ-above-culture approach permits activity in the wider world but places less value on that activity. As with the two-kingdoms theory, science, politics, and other secular fields can be understood

---

10. See Niebuhr, *Christ and Culture.*

through careful application of reason. However, religious pursuits are viewed as a higher calling than secular pursuits.

The Christ-and-culture-in-paradox approach is similar to the Christ-above-culture approach, but it places greater emphasis on the fallen or corrupt nature of the social and natural worlds. From this perspective, the social and natural worlds are not to be avoided, but there is also a sense that they cannot be perfected or elevated (to use Aquinas's language), making the study of these areas less valuable. Christians need to "play by the rules of the game" within the secular world, but they tend to avoid or withdraw from areas that seem particularly problematic or hard to square with Christian principles.

All three of these categories are consistent with nature-and-grace dualism, but each places slightly different value on (or has varying levels of concern about) engagement with the wider society. We will see later in the book that there are similar differences in the level of engagement some Christians have with the field of psychology.

Carson believes that both nature-and-grace dualism and the two-kingdoms theory can have significant benefits. In his view, both approaches see value in "earthly activities," allowing Christians to engage in science, civic life, politics, and so on without feeling as though they are doing something of lesser value. Indeed, Martin Luther stressed the value of all vocations and emphasized that engaging in so-called sacred activities did not bring one closer to God than being a lowly servant. In addition, at least two of these approaches highlight the unavoidable, and in many ways unresolvable, separation and even tension between the two worlds.

However, from Carson's point of view, these perspectives can also have a negative impact because they lead to separating everyday life from the sacred or religious life. As a result, science can be studied through a relatively neutral process; civic life is relatively separate from the life of the church. The church's impact on society relates primarily to ethical or moral issues, which Carson suggests gives the church a very minor role in the activities of society and reduces the impact of the gospel. In addition, in the realm of science and scholarship, these views lead to disjointed knowledge. He states, "If we then apply such a polarized two kingdoms theory to every domain of human endeavor, we shall not even attempt a unifying approach to knowledge: there will be knowledge grounded in human reason, and knowledge grounded in revelation and faith, and the two will not meet."[11] Carson's concern is that disconnected knowledge leads to a split personality and is intellectually unsatisfying because all the pieces of the puzzle do not seem to fit together. In addition, this disconnection results in Christians having very little meaningful impact on science, civic society, or cultural activities.

Of course, the actual practice of individuals is certainly not as homogeneous as the three approaches of Niebuhr suggest, and there are variations on how these ideas might be applied to real-world issues. You may identify with some of these perspectives, but you may also find yourself applying them in ways that don't match the concerns expressed by Carson or others.

How might these views influence an approach to psychology? Embracing a strong separation between the secular or natural world and the sacred or religious world leads to treating psychological science as a relatively neutral endeavor that can be understood through observation and reason. Since reasoning is inherent in all human beings, even nonbelievers can arrive at the same earthly truth. While grace (i.e., faith applied by those who are redeemed) may elevate or perfect this process, it ultimately does not change the process. Those who embrace these perspectives may believe that objectivity through clear reasoning is important in all fields of science, including psychology, and that specific theological or religious perspectives should be kept out of the process. Religious issues enter the realm of psychology only when specific moral or ethical questions conflict with scientific findings. In chapter 7 we will discuss both the potential benefits and some of the difficulties that may arise from this approach when applied to psychology.

Grace in Opposition to Nature

A second major view concerning the relationship between the natural world (including the physical and social worlds) and the spiritual world is grace in opposition to nature. Niebuhr coined the phrase

11. Carson, *Christ and Culture Revisited*, 211.

"Christ against culture," which he described as either a separation from the wider culture or a battle with it. This view goes back many centuries, and many strains of thought have contributed to it. Gnosticism, a first-century philosophy that viewed the material world as flawed or evil, is perhaps one such influence. Some of the basis for this idea can be traced to the Greek philosopher Plato, who saw the material world as transient and significantly inferior to the spiritual world (i.e., the world of the ethereal soul). Full embrace of Gnosticism, adopted by some early Christian and Jewish sects, was considered a heresy by many in the early church. However, aspects of this notion morphed and lived on throughout the centuries in many different forms, and strains of the idea have influenced Christians in a variety of ways.[12] One version of this influence contributed to the monastic tradition described earlier.

Anabaptist view. Another version shaped, to some degree, the views of the Anabaptists (not to be confused with Christians who call themselves Baptists). Early adherents to this movement focused a great deal on a withdrawal from society and culture. This withdrawal was due in part to theological perspectives but also to severe persecution experienced by many in this movement during the early sixteenth century. Elements of this view continue today in a variety of forms and in differing Christian groups including the Amish, Mennonites, and several others.

Many contemporary descendants of Anabaptist traditions do not flee from all forms of cultural engagement. For example, John Howard Yoder, a more recent Mennonite theologian, strongly objected to the characterization of Anabaptists as being against culture.[13] He argued that Christians need to be countercultural and not necessarily withdrawn from culture and that Anabaptists exemplify this better than most groups. Yoder wrote that Christians should avoid cultural trends, such as consumerism, autonomous reason, and blind obedience to the state. Thus, while Anabaptists still engage less with some elements of society, they attempt to shape many elements of the culture—primarily by displaying or exemplifying an alternative way of living.

---

12. Brown and Strawn, *Physical Nature of Christian Life*, 23–27.
13. See Marshall, "Overview of Christ and Culture."

Fundamentalism. Christian fundamentalism shares some but not all the features of the Anabaptist perspective. This point of view is not clearly identified with a specific denomination or theological tradition but cuts across many groups. While a precise definition of Christian fundamentalism is difficult, there are at least three main features of this perspective: (1) a strong adherence to the inerrancy and infallibility of Scripture, (2) opposition to the perceived immorality of contemporary culture and a strong desire to steer the wider society toward a Christian ethic and piety, and (3) opposition to liberalism (i.e., lacking openness to new ideas and social progress) and some forms of modernity (e.g., social and religious diversity).[14] According to Carson, the movement—particularly among North American Christians—differs from the form of separation of Anabaptists in that

> much of this cultural engagement is reactive: fundamentalists spot di-
> rections being taken by the broader culture that they feel are immoral
> or dangerous and adopt strategies to confront them and if possible
> overturn them. At the risk of generalization, they are reasonably ef-
> fective at combating what they do not like in the culture even while
> exhibiting relatively little interest in the ways one should support the
> culture, working into the worlds of art and music. A substantial part of
> the appeal is to tradition: America may not be a Christian nation, they
> say, but it was founded on Christian principles—and the movement
> itself is an appeal to return to such Christian principles.[15]

This approach does not promote avoiding all engagement with the wider world, but as Herman Bavinck, a critic of fundamentalism, states, "Never do we find here genuine, true, full reformation; there is only a rescuing and snatching of individuals out of the world which lies in wickedness; never a methodical, organic reformation of the whole, of the cosmos, of the nation and country. In all these movements there is an attack on the component parts, not on the centre; on the ramparts, not on the fortress itself."[16]

---

14. See Bendroth, "Christian Fundamentalism in America."
15. Carson, *Christ and Culture Revisited*, 209.
16. Veenhof, "Nature and Grace in Bavinck," 17.

For supporters and admirers of this view, fundamentalism represents an attempt to remain true to the foundations of Christian faith, to maintain the essentials of the gospel message, and to promote the need for piety and faithful living. For critics and detractors, this view represents a form of fleeing from the world. It does little to engage with the broader society in a constructive way and limits the Christian life to a small set of pious practices.

How do these ideas relate to the interaction between faith and psychology? As we will describe in chapter 6, taking a grace-over-nature position often leads individuals to keep a relatively safe distance from the discipline of psychology. This can lead to open antagonism toward the discipline at one end of the continuum, or, at the other, potentially feeling that Christians should (to paraphrase Bavinck and potentially overstate the issue) snatch what is good out of the wickedness that is the entire discipline.

It needs to be said that, as Margaret Bendroth noted when tracing the history of Christian fundamentalism, individuals in this movement were not necessarily against all science. She suggests that many fundamentalists in the mid-twentieth century adopted a Scottish "common sense" philosophy, believing that "it was possible to know true things about the world through an innate capacity of perception."[17] Interestingly, this idea was applied not only to the natural world but also to Scripture, which they felt could be understood using observation and reason. Thus, while scientific theories about evolution or other findings deemed to be in opposition to Christian faith were rejected, some fundamentalists embraced many scientific findings—particularly in the natural sciences. As a result, some from this background find value in specific psychological findings or practices while also finding many of the perspectives within the discipline to be antithetical to Christian piety and practice.

Grace Renews Nature

The final approach concerning nature and grace is exemplified by Niebuhr's last category: Christ the transformer of culture. He felt this approach was promoted by the early church theologian Augustine and

17. Bendroth, "Christian Fundamentalism in America."

the later church reformer John Calvin. It is the one Niebuhr favored. This approach has often been associated with churches in the reformed tradition (i.e., churches formed as part of the Reformation that follow the teachings of reformers such as John Calvin and John Knox), despite the fact that there is wide variation in adherence to this view within reformed churches.

This approach, like the two-kingdoms idea, suggests that the earthly kingdom is affected by sin and that the natural world does not function as originally intended (i.e., disease, suffering, and death were not intended). However, the approach differs from the two-kingdoms theory in two ways. First, in this view, even human reason is distorted by sin, which can lead humans to a very incorrect understanding of reality. For example, learning that genetic factors can influence intelligence led some scientists and psychologists in the early twentieth century to embrace eugenics.[18] This idea promoted the practice of selective breeding of human populations to "improve" humanity. It also lent support to racist ideologies, including the rationale that was used by Nazis to exterminate Jews and that influenced laws in America enforcing sterilization of "undesirables." Thus, a distorted interpretation of data led directly to an evil outcome.

A second way this approach differs from the two-kingdoms concept is that adherents are to go beyond operating within the world as neutral players. They are to be agents of change—both for the natural world and for the social world. The late nineteenth-century Dutch theologians Herman Bavinck and Abraham Kuyper expanded on John Calvin's views on society by providing a road map for how Christians should engage with the wider culture. Both men saw value in the natural world and in the natural order of the world, despite their being distorted by the curse of sin. Bavinck stated that sin "is not a substance, . . . it is not the essence of things, but rather adheres to the essence; . . . and to that extent contingent, an alien intruder like death. It can therefore be isolated from the essence and removed from it. The world is and remains susceptible to purification and deliverance. Its essence can be saved, and its original state can return."[19]

18. See Kevles, "Eugenics and Human Rights."
19. Veenhof, "Nature and Grace in Bavinck," 20.

Both Bavinck and Kuyper saw value in science, art, politics, and cultural engagement, but in doing these activities, Christians were called to restore them to their original form. Kuyper's rather famous statement sums up his approach: "Oh, no single piece of our mental world is to be hermetically sealed off from the rest, and there is not a square inch in the whole domain of our human existence over which Christ, who is sovereign over all, does not cry, 'Mine'!"[20] Carson elaborates by stating, "Because all truth is God's truth, because nothing we legitimately study is unrelated to Christ, Kuyper felt compelled to demonstrate how Christ's sovereignty operates in every sphere."[21] In this view, there is less of a sacred/secular divide than is inherent in the two-kingdoms approach. Therefore, all academic pursuits, political activities, business, cultural activities, and such were open to Christians, but they also needed "restoration." Kuyper believed in a pluralistic approach to society in which Christian institutions (e.g., Christian political parties, Christian schools, Christian labor unions, etc.) would compete with other worldviews within the larger marketplace of ideas.

Of course, there are many supporters as well as critics of Niebuhr's favored view and of Kuyper's "every square inch" approach (which are similar but certainly not identical). For supporters, these approaches allow Christians to feel comfortable working in various fields without feeling that their work is of less value. These approaches contain an inspiring message of change and transformation. They also attract many Christians who value science, culture, politics, art, and academic pursuits while still identifying much that needs to be changed. Finally, supporters point to the unity of knowledge that may be lacking in other worldviews, since "all truth is God's truth."

Critics (including some from within the tradition) have accused adherents of being triumphalist. In other words, they are overly optimistic about what can be accomplished, and the movement gives the impression that to be a truly "successful Christian" one must dramatically transform some area of society. Some writers from within the Reformed tradition have raised concerns that attempts to transform

20. Kuyper, *Abraham Kuyper*, 488.
21. Carson, *Christ and Culture Revisited*, 214.

society may sometimes backfire. As one Reformed blogger suggested, in speaking positively about his Anabaptist brothers and sisters in Christ, "They recognize that, often, the church that tries to change the world eventually becomes a church the world has changed."[22] Also, as Carson points out, many critics point to the simple fact that—unlike in Kuyper's era—it is impossible to adopt a Kuyperian approach when so much of the contemporary world is controlled by those who do not recognize the lordship of Jesus Christ.

Those who take a more reformational view of culture tend to embrace psychological science as both valid and valuable, but they also seek to apply Christian worldviews to shape the discipline. This shaping process can take on a variety of forms as will be described in chapter 8. Here we will simply say that for some this means applying broad perspectives when interpreting data while leaving much of psychological science and practice as they are. For others, it means a more radical or complete transformation of the discipline by restructuring it from the ground up.

Views of the Person

In addition to views on nature and grace, religious views of the person and a person's relationship to God can also significantly impact one's approach to psychology.

The Nature of Sin

All Christian groups speak of sin, but groups vary concerning the doctrine of original sin. Following the lead of Augustine, the Roman Catholic Church and the majority of Protestant groups teach that all humans are inherently sinful from birth—in other words, prone to evil by "nature" and therefore in need of salvation.[23] Protestants who follow the church reformer John Calvin take this a bit further with the doctrine of total depravity, which suggests that no human can do any good, in thought, word, or deed, at least from a divine perspective (i.e.,

22. Wax, "3 Reasons."
23. See Vawter, "Original Sin."

humans can do good deeds in the eyes of others but not in the eyes of God).[24] However, groups such as Eastern Orthodox churches[25] and most Anabaptists[26] believe that a corrupted society or culture and the deficient nature of our being mean that we have a strong tendency to desire sin—but only when we act on that sin are we sinful.

Another issue regarding the theology of sin is the personal or collective nature of sin. For some groups, sin is very much a personal trait or a personal failing. For other groups, sin is part of the brokenness of the world that came after the willful disobedience of humans. This brokenness encompasses willful, conscious sins; unconscious sins; sins of omission; sin due to a distorted human nature; the collective sin of groups and institutions; and even a distortion of the natural world (i.e., disease and death). Brokenness involves distorted thinking and distorted structures that pervade groups, governments, and whole societies.[27] One example of this type of brokenness is institutional racism. This is often cited as an example of sin that is not conscious or willful but exists as part of a broken system that ultimately has a very negative impact on individuals from a certain group.

Agency and God's Providence

While many Christians speak of "God's plan," we don't all think the same way about how human or personal history unfolds. For some, mostly those from a Calvinist or Lutheran perspective, God directs human affairs to a great extent—even to the point of determining in advance who is saved and who is not (often called the doctrine of predestination).[28] In this view, we are simply called to respond with thanksgiving if we experience salvation. We cannot achieve this salvation through actions or even through our personally initiated belief. Thus, we are not determined by natural forces (as some psychologists propose). Rather, our lives are planned for us in advance by God. However, other Christians place greater emphasis on free will and personal

24. See Baschera, "Total Depravity?"
25. See Benz, *Eastern Orthodox Church.*
26. See Finger, *Contemporary Anabaptist Theology.*
27. See Wolters, *Creation Regained.*
28. See Boettner, *Reformed Doctrine of Predestination.*

responsibility. For some with this latter perspective, this emphasis applies mostly to salvation (i.e., we choose God rather than God choosing us). For others, the notion of free will extends to nearly all everyday choices (i.e., we make free, uninfluenced choices toward good or evil).

The issue of miracles is another way God's providence enters into the discussion of God's involvement in our lives. Most Christians hold out the possibility that God intervenes in the natural world through special means that do not follow the normal course of events. However, there is great variation as to how frequent or common this is. On one end of the continuum, miracles are a nearly daily occurrence. On the other end of the spectrum, miracles are very rare or perhaps occurred only during Bible times.[29] Those on this end of the continuum are often concerned that Christians view gaps in our knowledge about natural events as being God's action, while the rest of the natural order runs on its own. These same individuals argue that this "God of the gaps" notion is dangerous, because as science is able to explain more and more phenomenon, the gaps begin to shrink to the point that we no longer need God to explain anything.[30] According to these Christians, God's action in the world does not normally violate the natural order. Rather, he works through the natural order (e.g., "It *seems* like a miracle that the doctors were able to save the patient").

Body/Soul Dualism

Finally, there are different perspectives on the nature of our bodily existence. As we discussed in chapter 2 (and in the appendix), some Christians believe that humans are made of two substances: body and soul. According to this dualism, the "real person" resides in the soul, and the body is simply a vessel for the soul.[31] This view sees conscious and rational thought, moral decision making, and spiritual direction as being directly tied to the soul, while the body leads us astray through the desires of the sinful flesh. This view is not identical to the nature-and-grace dualism described earlier, but it has similar elements. A more

29. See Del Colle, "Miracles in Christianity."
30. See Larmer, "Is There Anything Wrong with 'God of the Gaps' Reasoning?"
31. See Cooper, *Body, Soul, and Life Everlasting.*

negative view of the natural world coincides with a more negative view of the material nature of humans.

Other Christians have challenged this view, suggesting that the sins of the flesh reside not in the flesh itself but in our corrupted nature. Therefore, our bodies are viewed as broken but redeemable. These Christians place greater emphasis on the role the body plays in our everyday actions and even within the Christian life.[32]

Implications for Psychology

The theological issues described above do not necessarily correlate with each other, and within one group or individual, there can be a wide range of conclusions about the various issues. With that caveat in mind, we can examine certain beliefs and envision how they might influence responses to psychological theories and practices.

Imagine a Christian student beginning the study of psychology who has the following set of views. First, her view of sin focuses on the personal and downplays systemic brokenness. Second, she believes that individuals exercise a great deal of free will in response to God's call to believe as well as to live in obedience. Third, she emphasizes the life of the Spirit and believes that, while the world is God's world, it is also a place of great temptation and evil thinking. Finally, she believes that humans are of two substances and that the soul is the seat of thought, moral direction, and willful action. This individual will tend to have a relatively negative view of the discipline of psychology. Why? Because psychology emphasizes causal influences on behavior and either rejects or downplays free will and personal responsibility for actions. She will see psychology as dominated by secular thought and therefore a potential source of temptation toward un-Christian thinking. Finally, if the soul is the seat of consciousness and willful action, then how can psychology even be a science (i.e., study something that is not subject to natural laws), and how can psychologists claim that people with a biological disorder are unable to control their own behavior when the soul should be able to overrule the flesh?

32. See Wolters, *Creation Regained.*

Another Christian interested in psychology has the following views. First, he views sin as primarily a systemic problem that has less to do with individual personal failings or bad moral choices. Second, he believes in free will but also heavily emphasizes God's sovereignty and foreknowledge (i.e., seeing God as directing much or all of human outcomes). Third, he emphasizes intellectual belief in God more than emotional or spiritual enlightenment and feels that, while human reason is not perfect, through proper application of reason, a person can understand much about God and the world. Finally, he leans toward viewing the person as a unity and not comprised of two substances. This person is much more likely to fully embrace psychological science and practice because he sees no significant discrepancy between some of the deterministic views in psychology and the notion of God's providential work in the world. He may see psychology as something relatively neutral apart from religious notions or perhaps something that is broadly shaped by religious ideas. Finally, he will embrace the science of the mind, since predictability of mental states and behavior seems compatible with a natural science approach applied to social science.

Finally, a third Christian interested in psychology has a strong belief in nature-and-grace dualism. She believes that the natural world is not inherently sinful or broken, but it is of much less value than the spiritual or the sacred. She believes strongly in the dual nature of human beings but also sees the body as an important element of the person and something that can constrain a person's ability to act in certain ways. The natural world can be studied in a relatively neutral manner, but the spiritual world operates in a very different way—even though the spiritual world can impact the natural world through miracles or through our own mental processes. She believes strongly in free will and personal responsibility but also that society or our own bodies can powerfully impact our thinking and behavior. This student may be relatively comfortable with some aspects of psychological science but see others as being either incomplete (e.g., not acknowledging the spiritual or the miraculous) or incompatible (e.g., claiming specific external causes when in fact an action was willful). This student may dutifully study the findings and practices of psychology but may also want to reorient or even reinvent many ideas in psychology to incorporate more of the spiritual nature of the person.

These three descriptions are fictitious, and we cannot assume that holding one theological or philosophical view will automatically coincide with another view. We also cannot say that having a set of beliefs always leads to certain views of psychology. However, hopefully these illustrations show how a person's theological tradition can impact their leanings in psychology. Perhaps they will also help you identify the way you approach psychology or how you may wish to approach it in the future. Chapters 5–8 will unpack these influences further when applying these views to specific models.

QUESTIONS FOR DISCUSSION

1. Think about your own personal history or religious beliefs. How does your religious tradition view the issues described in this chapter? Were you fully aware of these views, completely unaware and uninfluenced by these views, or unaware but still unconsciously influenced by these views?

2. How have your views about engagement with the wider society, as well as issues concerning sin, agency, embodiment, and such, influenced your general acceptance of psychological science?

3. How should Christians respond when contemporary culture, the wider society, or even the scientific community rejects any influence from religious ideas? In other words, how can you be true to your faith but still work in this world?

PART 2

MODELS OF INTEGRATION

The first part of this book provided the "what" and the "where" of worldviews—as in, "What are different epistemologies?" and "Where do our ideas about psychology and faith originate?" But we now turn our attention to the "how" of worldviews—as in, "How have various Christians related their faith to psychology?" As you already saw in previous chapters, several different approaches exist, and these ideas and approaches have also evolved over time. As we examine the different approaches, we will provide illustrations of how worldviews influence one's approach to integration.

People have offered various schemes to describe and categorize approaches to relating psychology and Christianity. An early attempt by John Carter and Bruce Narramore used the categories of *Against* (psychology against religion and vice versa), *Of* (psychology of religion), *Parallels* (psychology and theology as important but ultimately separate endeavors), and *Integrates* (psychology and theology influence one another).[1] *Psychology and Christianity: Five Views*, edited by Eric Johnson, breaks up attempts at integration using the categories of *biblical counseling, levels of explanation, integration, transformative*, and *Christian psychology*.

While the way models are grouped and named varies among authors, there are consistent themes that arise in making these distinctions. Many models attempt to take a stance on two dimensions: (1) the utility of science for understanding human behavior and (2) the utility of theology for understanding human behavior.[2] The framework we propose uses these two dimensions to help people locate their own approach to the interface of psychology and Christianity. One dimension, the utility of science, recognizes that people differ in terms of how useful they see scientific psychology for understanding human nature and addressing human problems. Some advocates believe that psychology is an extremely powerful tool for this task, while others question its usefulness. The second dimension, the utility of theology, recognizes that people vary in terms of how useful they think Christianity is for understanding human behavior and problems. Some view Christian theology as an important means for addressing human nature, while others view religion as an impediment to doing so. We can combine these dimensions into a chart on which different approaches to integration can be placed (see fig. 1).

As mentioned above, people have offered various models of integration. So why add another one? First, our model seeks to organize disparate forms of integration using common dimensions. This allows one to more easily compare models and see how they relate to one another. Second, our model shows that forms of integration exist on a continuum and acknowledges that people may not fall neatly into one category or another. Many may find themselves in between different integrative approaches, so reducing integration approaches to a handful of categories is somewhat artificial.

1. See Carter and Narramore, *Integration of Psychology and Theology*.
2. We are using the term *theology* throughout the book as including formal theology (i.e., systematic study of Scripture), basic biblical principles, and broader religious worldviews.

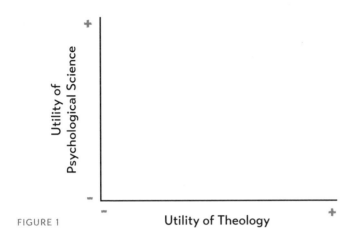

FIGURE 1   **Utility of Theology**

Part 2 of this book examines different models of integration using the two dimensions described above. Chapter 5 examines scientific reductionism, an approach that has a high view of psychology but a low view of Christianity. Chapter 6 looks at biblical reductionism, an approach that sees Christian theology as being valuable for understanding human nature but tends to downplay the utility of psychological science. Chapter 7 examines what we broadly call complementary models of integration. These approaches value both theology and psychology but differ in some of the details about how the two should interact. The three complementary approaches that we consider are territorialism, perspectivalism, and integrationism. Chapter 8 centers on the final model of integration we will be examining: humanizers of science. This model is a bit unique in that it doesn't just seek to bring psychological science and Christian theology together but rather argues for a redefinition of what is included under the umbrella of psychology. Humanizers are not dismissive of contemporary psychology but believe that a broader definition is needed that includes the contributions of theology.

Using the dimensions introduced above, we attempt to describe these models and place them on a continuum (see fig. 2). Of course, this is an imperfect process, and there may be some disagreement among adherents of each model as to where their model should fall.

Furthermore, since we are dealing with continuums here, some people may fall in between models. Nonetheless, we feel that it's useful to map out some of the more common approaches to see how they relate to one another.

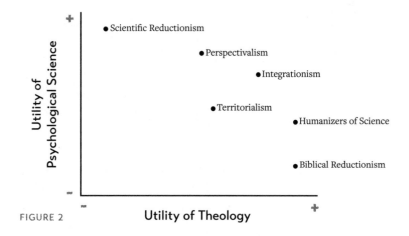

FIGURE 2

5

Scientific Reductionism

Consider this quotation: "The moral worldview of any scientifically literate person—one who is not blinkered by fundamentalism—requires a radical break from religious conceptions of meaning and value."[1] This quotation from well-known Harvard University psychologist Steven Pinker is representative of contemporary versions of scientific reductionism. This chapter focuses on psychologists who have a high view of scientific psychology but a low view of theology for explaining behavior. Extreme forms of this view often result in a total rejection of a Christian worldview, while in other forms it manifests as merely downplaying the role of religion in psychology.

Reductionism is the belief that higher-level phenomena can be fully explained by or reduced to lower-level processes. For example, reductionism would claim that emotions can be fully reduced to a biological explanation (i.e., an interaction of the peripheral and central nervous systems) or that complex altruistic behavior can be reduced to an evolutionary explanation. While scientific exploration legitimately seeks to simplify complex phenomena, reductionism goes beyond simplification to a more deterministic account of behavior. This view

1. Pinker, "Science Is Not Your Enemy."

often discounts other explanations for human behavior, including agency (i.e., free will), divine actions, or spiritual forces. Reductionism views the integration of psychological and theological explanations for human behavior as both unnecessary and—as the opening quotation suggests—potentially harmful to psychological science. From a psychological reductionist standpoint, religion and theology can be reduced to psychological factors and therefore offer nothing unique in understanding human behavior. Psychology can explain away religion, and therefore theology is not afforded an equal footing. Reductionistic claims rely on the assumption that science is the only tool equipped to answer questions about human nature. Some lip service may be paid to the utility of philosophy and theology, but both are viewed as interesting speculations.

There have been different forms of reductionism in the history of psychology, with Freud reducing behavior to unconscious processes, Skinner reducing behavior to environmental reinforcements, and others reducing behavior to biological factors. This latter form—sometimes called material reductionism—suggests that the mind can be reduced to the biological functions of the brain, such that mental processes (e.g., cognition, emotion) are nothing but physical processes. More recently, evolutionary psychologists have viewed human thought and behavior as explainable in terms of things that would enable our ancestors to pass on their genes. What many of these forms have in common is their rejection of religion as a source of truth or of spiritual factors as explanatory. Instead, religion and spirituality are seen as phenomena that need to be explained by lower-level processes.

Some in modern psychology reject unqualified reductionism because they see behavior as multifaceted and not necessarily reducible to one process (e.g., the unconscious, conditioning; see chaps. 1–3 for additional discussion). However, there is still a tendency to reduce human behavior to something that can be explained via empirical science. Many recognize that we are more than just our environment and more than just our genes (nature *and* nurture rather than nature *versus* nurture), but the dominant current view sees human nature as reducible to biology, environment, and the interaction between the two. Otto Fenichel sums this up, stating that "scientific psychology explains mental phenomena as a result of the interplay of primitive physical needs—rooted in biological structure of man and developed in the course of biological history . . .—and the influences of the environment on these needs. There is no place for any third factor."[2]

Two examples of scientific reductionism in psychology are radical behaviorism and evolutionary psychology. Radical behaviorism will serve as a historical example, while evolutionary psychology is a more contemporary demonstration. How do these viewpoints approach human nature? How do they view religion and its contributions?

Radical Behaviorism

B. F. Skinner is often ranked as one of the most influential psychologists in the history of psychology and is best known for his contributions to a school of thought called behaviorism.[3] As discussed in chapter 3, behaviorism is the theory that behavior is shaped through the environment via learning processes. Skinner focused most of his work on operant conditioning and believed that virtually all behaviors are shaped through a series of rewards and punishments. A robust body of evidence supports the effectiveness of operant conditioning in altering the behavior of animals and humans alike.[4] However, Skinner took behaviorism to an extreme position, sometimes called radical behaviorism. In addition to environmental influences, Skinner claimed that mental events were not causal in nature—that is, mental events do not cause behavior and in fact are epiphenomenal (i.e., a by-product of brain activity). So, our consciousness or "inner events" are merely side effects of our conditioning and are not ultimately responsible for directing our actions. As he put it, "We do not act because we feel like acting. . . . We act *and* feel like acting for a common reason to be sought in our environmental history."[5]

Therefore, radical behaviorism reduces human behavior to environmental influences, leaving no explanatory power to mental

2. Fenichel, *Psychoanalytic Theory of Neurosis*, 5.
3. See Haggbloom et al., "100 Most Eminent Psychologists."
4. For a review, see Staddon and Cerutti, "Operant Conditioning."
5. Skinner, *Reflections on Behaviorism and Society*, 51.

events.[6] Skinner argued that just as our views of physical events as being "from the gods" or from other supernatural forces were replaced with scientific explanations (e.g., physics, chemistry), so our understanding of human behavior should move from vague explanations of things like free will to more empirical explanations.[7] If people wish to know why I (Blake) chose to be a psychologist, they should not ask me for a narrative about my motives. Rather, they should identify those reinforcers and/or punishments that pushed me in that direction. Perhaps I was rewarded by good grades in an early psychology class, or maybe some expressed interest was supported by my parents or authority figures. Likewise, if I struggled in other academic areas, this may have driven me away from other areas of study. Skinner would dismiss any narrative explanation I might come up with, such as "I really desired this" or "I thought psychology was intriguing." These thoughts would be seen as epiphenomenal in nature and not causes of my behavior.

Skinner saw conditioning and reinforcement both as the reason for social problems (e.g., aggression) and as the solution. In a televised interview, Skinner demonstrates many of the principles of operant conditioning by showing pigeons engaged in a variety of tasks that would not come naturally to pigeons (including playing a form of table tennis!).[8] The pigeons were conditioned to do these various tasks, but one of the more interesting points comes toward the end of the interview. Skinner discusses pigeons that were conditioned to attack each other when a green light was on but not when a white light was on. Pigeons are normally nonaggressive, but these pigeons were rewarded with a food pellet for being aggressive when the light was green but not when the light was white. Skinner then relates this to human aggression, stating, "There are many instances in which one is reinforced for attacking another and in the 'world of the green light,' where that

6. Behaviorism in general focuses on the importance of studying observable behavior rather than internal mental events because the latter are unobservable. Radical behaviorism goes a step further with the addition of a philosophical assumption: not only are mental events not observable, but they also do not have causal force on behavior.

7. Skinner, *Beyond Freedom and Dignity*, 5–10.

8. Skinner, *Learning and Behavior*.

reinforcement prevails we will always have problems of aggression. There is a possibility that we can construct some kind of 'world of the white light' in which no one is reinforced for being aggressive and just the possibility in that case we wouldn't have the problem of aggression."[9]

It is important to notice that Skinner is reducing aggression and non-aggression to schedules (i.e., patterns) of reinforcement. As with other phenomena, Skinner has no interest in the internal mental processes that underlie aggression. Aggression is a problem that developed due to external factors and reinforcement, and therefore it must be solved in the same way.

For radical behaviorism, religion does not uniquely contribute to an understanding of human behavior. To be sure, it might be an environmental factor used to explain behavior. For example, certain behaviors such as generosity and charity may have been reinforced for someone who grew up in a Christian household, which then increases the likelihood of future charitable giving. However, under the radical behaviorism framework, this means that religion and theology are simply environmental factors that conditioned the person to act charitably. Issues of morality, purpose, and meaning in life are seen as matters of social contract and not things that objectively exist outside oneself. Skinner argued that we should focus on shaping our environment, rather than on ethics and moral reasoning, to create desirable behaviors.[10] In other words, morality and religion can be reduced to a set of situational contingencies that can be completely explained by behaviorist principles.

While radical behaviorism is not a predominant view in contemporary psychology, elements of this view remain as unspoken assumptions in cognitive-behavioral approaches and cognitive neuroscience.

Evolutionary Psychology

Another form of scientific reductionism can be seen in certain versions of evolutionary psychology. Evolutionary psychology (see chap. 3 for

9. Skinner, *Learning and Behavior*.
10. Skinner, *Reflections on Behaviorism and Society*, 52.

additional background) assumes that genetic variations allowing an organism to pass on its genes will be favored. Therefore, one way to examine various human behaviors is to see how they may be related to psychological patterns that allowed our ancestors to survive. This does not mean that all human behavior is adaptive to our current circumstances, since culture changes faster than genes. However, our behavior is rooted in the past in our ability to survive and pass on our genes.

Evolutionary frameworks have been used to explain both behaviors and mental events, where everything from food preferences to emotional experiences (e.g., love, fear) to group-based behaviors (e.g., competition, cooperation) may be rooted in our evolutionary history. For example, cooperation and altruism within groups may have developed because natural selection favored those who worked together and cared for others, making them or their offspring more likely to survive, thus securing the survival of their genes.[11] As Heather Looy, a biopsychologist and Christian, puts it, "Many evolutionary psychologists claim that evolutionary psychology provides a powerful and virtually complete account of human nature, including ontological and teleological questions—a meta-narrative of breathtaking proportions."[12] In other words, many evolutionary psychological accounts seek to go beyond explaining a specific behavior and attempt to make sweeping claims about the nature and purpose of human beings in general.

Evolutionary explanations have gained prominence within the field of psychology over the past few decades and have been applied to a variety of subdisciplines, including social, developmental, and cognitive psychology. As Todd Shackelford and James Liddle state, "Evolutionary psychology is best viewed as an approach to psychology rather than a subdiscipline of psychology. Evolutionary psychologists are not limited to studying particular topics such as social behavior, cognitive development, or personality; an evolutionary perspective can be

---

11. For a review, see Kurzban, Burton-Chellew, and West, "Evolution of Altruism in Humans."

12. Looy, "Sex Differences," 301.

applied to any area of psychological research. Evolutionary psychology is uniquely suited to provide a unifying theoretical framework for the currently disparate subdisciplines of psychology."[13]

In this framework, religion is something to be studied but not something that should have a direct impact on our understanding of human nature. It is either a predictor variable (How does religiosity predict prosocial behavior?) or something to be explained using empirical science (How is religion a way of making meaning?). Whether or not the religion is true doesn't enter into the equation. While theology speaks to issues of ultimate meaning and morality, evolutionary psychology attempts to reduce these areas to evolutionary drives.

Evolutionary Psychology and Religion

Evolutionary psychologists suggest that religion must be adaptive since it is found in virtually every culture. According to some, religion may be adaptive because it facilitates cooperation and trust.[14] Religion offers a set of precepts and rules that may encourage and enforce cooperation with in-group members. This in turn helps the group as a whole to thrive and genes to be passed on. Of course, history has shown that religion can also create conflict between groups. The evolutionary explanation for this conflict is that the benefits of cooperation should be shared with only the immediate in-group to be most effective. Cooperating with out-group members would not yield as many benefits and would take resources away from the in-group. Therefore, it may have been adaptive to dehumanize or isolate out-groups, and so religion may have served as a tool to promote both cooperation and conflict. Now, this is certainly an overly simplified example of the evolutionary view of religion, and some admit that the picture may be quite a bit more complex. Evolutionary psychologist Lee Kirkpatrick argues that this rather simplistic "good for the group" explanation may be inadequate from a modern evolutionary perspective and that evolutionary explanations require an enhancement of individual-level inclusive fitness as well as

---

13. Shackelford and Liddle, "Understanding the Mind," 254.
14. Bulbulia, "Cognitive and Evolutionary Psychology of Religion," 664–72.

group-level benefits.[15] However, both simplified evolutionary explanations and complex ones often reduce religion to an evolved behavior.

Another potential evolutionary factor in the development of religion is what anthropologist Stewart Guthrie describes as the human
tendency to ascribe agency to events that occur in the world.[16] Some
have called this tendency the Hyperactive Agency Detection Device
(HADD).[17] The tendency to ascribe agency to events can be seen as
adaptive. If a rock lands near you, it is more useful to assume that
someone threw it rather than that it just rolled off a pile of rocks. The
former assumption allows you to prepare for action (e.g., fight or flight),
while the latter would not focus your attention. Even if the falling rock
was not actually caused by an agent, the default assumption that it *was*
caused by someone would help you (and other organisms) survive.
What Guthrie and others argue is that while this HADD is adaptive, it
also causes humans to see causal agents where there are none. This in
turn leads humans to ascribe agency to things like storms, earthquakes,
and other natural events, and since the agents of these events cannot
be seen, this may eventually result in the belief in gods and/or spirits
that cause the events. Therefore, the human tendency to believe in God
(or gods) is reduced to an extension of the HADD.

Evolutionary Psychology and Morality

Morality is another area of religion affected by the reductionism
of evolutionary psychology. Most religions profess a form of moral
absolutism that suggests that most moral rules are universal and transcend human creation. Scientific reductionism rejects moral absolutes
because transcendent standards cannot be validated with observation.
Therefore, morality is viewed as a human construct or as something
constructed through evolutionary processes. E. O. Wilson was an evolutionary biologist who sought to explain transcendental concepts such
as religion and morality from an evolutionary perspective. He argued
that morality or, more accurately, our feelings of morality come from

---

15. Kirkpatrick, "Toward an Evolutionary Psychology," 927.
16. See Guthrie, *Faces in the Clouds*, 39–61.
17. Barret, "Cognitive Science, Religion, and Theology," 85–88.

biological processes honed over the course of our evolutionary history.[18] Therefore, our sense of morality came not from a transcendental source (top-down) but rather from biological realities (bottom-up). Wilson uses the example of adultery. A top-down perspective claims that adultery is wrong because it violates a principle God put into place. Adultery is wrong *a priori* and therefore feels wrong because we were created with an inherent sense of morality. A bottom-up argument claims that biological and environmental factors favored the development of some internal feeling promoting fidelity, since those with this feeling who then practiced monogamy were more likely to pass on their genes. The evolved feeling that adultery is wrong then led to people stating that adultery is wrong, and this belief eventually became codified in culture. In other words, adultery feels wrong not because it is morally wrong but because some adaptive mechanism made us believe it to be so.

Another example is seen in explanations of cooperation. Cooperation and beneficence may feel moral because those of our ancestors who cooperated were more likely to survive. Over time, this tendency, because it was shared by a large portion of the population, became codified into social structures. These codified rules are what we call morality or ethics, but in this framework biology is the ultimate cause rather than a transcendental source. As Wilson puts it, "The individual is seen as predisposed biologically to make certain choices. Through cultural evolution some of the choices are hardened into precepts, then into laws, and, if the predisposition or coercion is strong enough, into a belief in the command of God or the natural order of the universe."[19]

In summary, if religion and morality can be reduced to evolutionary explanations, then they offer no unique contribution to understanding human nature. They are something to be explained rather than something that offers explanations. Similar to what behaviorists would contend, theology does not offer any truths about human nature, values, or moral directions.

18. Wilson, "Biological Basis of Morality."
19. Wilson, "Biological Basis of Morality."

Worldview Foundations for Scientific Reductionism

As we turn toward an evaluation of scientific reductionism, we would first like to explore how this approach relates to worldview issues covered in the first part of the book. Much of scientific reductionism hinges on an epistemological assumption that the primary way to know truth is through empirical observation. In other words, positivism is the preferred approach, which suggests, as was described in chapter 1, that the scientific method is the best (and perhaps only) way to get at all truths about reality. In addition, this is typically accompanied by an ontology (i.e., the nature of reality) that all of nature—including humans—is part of a material world that follows natural laws that are knowable through observation. Related to this is an anthropology that sees humans as simply more advanced animals. Much of scientific reductionism emphasizes embodiment, and while scientific reductionists may acknowledge things like our relationality and our meaning-seeking nature, they often see these as merely more advanced versions of abilities that can be seen in other organisms. In essence, humans are not seen as being particularly special or distinct. In terms of axiology and teleology, scientific reductionists tend to see survival and the passing on of one's genes as the end goal of humanity, and, as discussed above, values and morals are seen as growing out of that rather than coming from a transcendental source (e.g., God).

An Evaluation of Scientific Reductionism

So, what are some strengths and weaknesses of the scientific reductionist approach? One strength is that it clearly takes scientific evidence seriously. Some Christians may be quick to dismiss scientific evidence that *seemingly* contradicts their worldview.[20] Yet as was described in previous chapters, most Christians in psychology believe that scientific evidence is something that needs to be understood and addressed. Therefore, the scientific findings coming out of a reduc-

---

20. We use the word *seemingly* because there are times when apparent contradictions between science and a Christian worldview are not actually contradictions but rather stem from a misunderstanding of either the scientific evidence or theology.

tionist perspective can be useful even if one rejects the underlying assumptions of reductionism.

In addition, the scientific reductionist approach pushes people toward an ethos of discovery. By seeking to explain complex phenomena like emotions, morality, and consciousness, the scientific method encourages new ways of examining behavior. For example, regardless of whether one agrees with Skinner's overall worldview, it is clear that he expanded our understanding of how reinforcers in the environment shape human behavior. Research on conditioning procedures has had a large impact on theory and applications in psychology. Some of these applications have been for good, like positive reinforcement in drug rehabilitation programs[21] or applied behavior analysis used to manage autism symptoms,[22] while others have been for ill, such as increasing the addictive nature of gambling devices.[23] Nonetheless, this ethos of discovery does push our understanding of human behavior forward in important ways.

However, despite these benefits, the reductionist approach has several weaknesses. In their push to use scientific psychology to understand human nature, scientific reductionists often make claims that go beyond the empirical data. Skinner's claims about a lack of free will go beyond the supporting data. Skinner himself admitted that neither view of behavior (free will or radical behaviorism) can be *proven*, though he believed that evidence supports the latter.[24]

It is important to realize that the reductionist narrative offers one interpretation of a given set of data, but there are other possible interpretations. For example, some evolutionary psychologists argue that the desire for a deity may be interpreted as a result of natural selection, because it is seen across cultures. However, an alternative explanation is that this is a result of us being made in the image of God. One's worldview, rather than data, seems to dictate which explanation is favored. One could even imagine a view that incorporates both explanations (e.g., God used evolutionary mechanisms to create this desire for a

21. Silverman, Holtyn, and Toegel, "Utility of Operant Conditioning."
22. Ringdahl, Kopelman, and Falcomata, "Applied Behavior Analysis."
23. Chóliz, "Experimental Analysis of the Game."
24. Skinner, *Beyond Freedom and Dignity*, 101.

deity). The question then becomes, Why should the reductionist account be the preferred one? The reductionist narrative may indeed be the correct one, but it must be evaluated alongside competing narratives. This doesn't mean we throw up our hands and say that all interpretations are equal. Rather, we examine and question the underlying assumptions of a given perspective to evaluate its claims. Is it logically consistent? Does it fit observable data? Do other narratives fit the data just as well? Heather Looy provides an example of this in her article examining sex differences through the lens of three frameworks: social constructionism, intelligent design, and evolutionary psychology.[25] She points out several assumptions of each viewpoint and shows that while evolutionary psychology offers one possible narrative, other narratives could also fit the observed data. The key point is that the narrative chosen depends as much on worldview as on empirical evidence. For all its claims of being based on empirical evidence, the evolutionary psychological perspective contains many assumptions that are not themselves empirically testable.

Another issue is that reductionistic views assume a single way of knowing or epistemology, and that is empirical science. This may result in what has been called scientism. C. Stephen Evans, a Christian philosopher, describes scientism as "the belief that all truth is scientific truth and that the sciences give us our best shot at knowing 'how things really are.'"[26] Of course, as described in chapter 1, empirical knowledge, while important, is not the only way of knowing something. While philosophy has acknowledged and attempted to deal with the limitations of positivism, psychology has yet to grapple with these issues and operates almost exclusively from a positivist framework (implicitly and explicitly).[27] Ironically, while focused on empirical, scientific knowledge as the primary way to understand the world, the scientific reductionist approach itself contains nonscientific assumptions. The reductionist says that the Christian view that objective morality exists and has its foundation in the nature and character of God is an unscientific claim (there is no way to prove or disprove it). Therefore, they

25. Looy, "Sex Differences."
26. Evans, *Preserving the Person*, 18.
27. Nelson, "Missed Opportunities in Dialogue," 212.

dismiss the narrative of objective morality, but this creates a problem. The reductionist is also using nonscientific assumptions. For example, they may be using a naturalist assumption that everything has a cause from (and only from) nature, but of course this statement itself is not something that can be determined empirically. The influence of non-scientific assumptions in scientific theories will be covered in greater depth in chapter 8.

Related to the issue of going beyond the empirical data is the fact that while many phenomena can be explained in a reductionistic way, this does not mean that the reductionist account fully explains a given phenomenon. For example, one could give a reductionistic account of a computer program by reducing it to binary code. In one sense, this would be comprehensive, since it could explain how the program works, but in another sense this explanation would be incomplete. The binary code cannot tell us the purpose of the program, how the program might be used, or whether the program is effective. The binary code is one level of explanation, but there are multiple levels. While this idea of levels of explanation will be developed more in chapter 7, it is important to note here that understanding a given phenomenon may require multiple levels, which makes reducing something to a single level problematic.

Donald MacKay was a neuroscientist who resisted the tendency to be overly reductionistic.[28] He warned against "nothing buttery"—the idea that one can say that mental activity is "nothing but" the firing of neurons. Mental activity may be embodied within the firing of neurons, but there is meaning beyond these mechanisms. There is a difference between saying that our emotions are related to areas in our limbic system and saying that our emotions are "nothing but" neural impulses. Does the emotion of love mean something beyond the firing of neurons? One could argue that human beings experience love only via the activation of brain circuits, but it doesn't necessarily follow that love is only the firing of those circuits. For example, if I (Blake Riek) am looking at an object (I'm currently looking at my phone), the way I see it is via light reflecting off it, entering my eye, and being processed

28. MacKay, "Brain Research and Human Responsibility," 40, 43.

and interpreted in my visual cortex. In one sense, my experience of the object can be explained as the firing of neurons in my visual system. However, that doesn't mean the object doesn't exist. My phone is a real object that I experience through my brain functions. In the same way, love can be a real phenomenon that I happen to experience through my brain functions. This is not a flawless argument, since I have other ways for assessing the reality of the phone, while it is unknown how one would measure love, but it illustrates the point that just because something can be explained at a neurological level doesn't mean that an understanding of that phenomenon can be reduced to that level.

Another weakness of reductionism is that it fails to allow for any moral grounding for its recommendations. Skinner advocated for the use of operant conditioning principles to improve environments (e.g., decrease aggression, help others) but struggled to define why this would be good. This is because his worldview doesn't allow for an objective "good" or "bad." As he puts it, "To make a value judgment by calling something good or bad is to classify it in terms of its reinforcing effects."[29] He wanted to create a "world of the white light," but it couldn't be grounded in any sense of objective morality. Additionally, his reductionist stance would require that he admit that his desire for this improved world was itself a result of conditioning, and therefore one could ask why he assumed this desire was good. In discussing values and good versus bad, Skinner didn't really move beyond the typical response that those things that allow survival are good. But why is survival in and of itself desirable? What if using "cruel" methods would increase survival?

Another problem with scientific reductionism can be seen in attempts to explain religion via reductionistic mechanisms. Many of those who fall in the reductionist camp tend to have simplistic or distorted views of what Christian theology teaches. Narramore points out that many psychologists "only have superficial contact with biblical Christianity, while others have had very negative encounters."[30] This was true when Narramore wrote it in 1973, and with the increasing

---

29. Skinner, *Beyond Freedom and Dignity*, 105.
30. Narramore, "Perspectives on the Integration of Psychology and Theology," 12.

secularization of society, it is likely even more true today.[31] Therefore, it shouldn't be surprising that religion is viewed skeptically by the psychological community and seen as something that must be psychologically explained.

It is easier to reduce or explain away religion when it is viewed simplistically. For example, in a speech to the Freedom from Religion Foundation, Steven Pinker stated, "Perhaps there really is a personal, attentive, invisible, miracle-producing, reward-giving, retributive deity, and we have a God module in order to commune with him. As a scientist, I like to interpret claims as testable hypotheses, and this certainly is one. It predicts, for example, that miracles should be observable, that success in life should be proportional to virtue, and that suffering should be proportional to sin. I don't know anyone who has done the necessary studies, but I would say there is good reason to believe that these hypotheses have not been confirmed."[32] But this is a simplistic and misrepresentative view of what Christian theology teaches. For example, Scripture makes it clear that following Christ can lead to persecution and even death (see Matt. 5:10–12; John 16:2), which is a far cry from Pinker's statement that "success in life should be proportional to virtue."

A final problem is that people may overgeneralize the similarities of religions to map an interesting evolutionary explanation. There is a degree of picking and choosing parts of a religion to fit the evolutionary narrative. For example, Kirkpatrick points out that religions have a common feature of in-group morality—its benefits are for the in-group. He uses the Old Testament command of loving your neighbor as an example of this and implies that this command would be applied only to other in-group members (i.e., Jews).[33] However, this ignores other parts of the Old Testament that call for benefiting the alien or foreigner, not to mention many similar passages in the New Testament. If one is allowed to pick and choose like this, almost any evolutionary story can be supported. It also speaks to the ignorance of religion that Narramore talked about.

31. G. Smith, "About Three-in-Ten US Adults Are Now Religiously Unaffiliated."
32. Pinker, "Evolutionary Psychology of Religion," 12.
33. Kirkpatrick, "Toward an Evolutionary Psychology," 939.

In summary, both the strengths and the weaknesses of this approach can be seen in the name of the approach itself: scientific reductionism. While the commitment to the scientific process is commendable, there are significant issues with the reductionist aspects of this approach. Yet to be against reductionism is not to reject the contributions of behaviorism or evolutionary psychology—or of similar reductionist attempts in the field—but to say that they are just one part of the picture rather than the whole.

QUESTIONS FOR DISCUSSION

1. Looking back at some of the psychological concepts you are familiar with (e.g., learning, emotion, cognitive development), what are some other examples of scientific reductionism in the field?

2. Can you think of ways in which both a Christian theological account and an evolutionary psychological account of something like love or morality may be true? In what sense may both provide valid insights? In what sense may they not?

6

Biblical Reductionism

Consider this quotation from a podcast produced by the Christian Counseling and Education Foundation (CCEF): "CCEF is committed to restoring Christ to counseling and counseling to the church."[1] This quotation is appealing for many students with a strong commitment to Christian faith, but what are the assumptions and implications of this view for the use of psychological science in a counseling setting? Is it legitimate for the church to be the primary provider of counseling services, or can non-Christian licensed therapists provide valuable treatment? Can psychological science be used even in a church counseling setting?

This chapter focuses on an approach to psychology that is roughly the opposite of the scientific reductionism discussed in the last chapter. In this case, psychology is reduced to theology, so we refer to this approach as biblical reductionism. Biblical reductionists value theology to explore and understand human nature but either dismiss or downplay psychological science as a tool for this endeavor. Biblical reductionists may value science for what it can tell us about the way the natural world

1. Groves and Stryd, "Methodology."

works, but they are skeptical that psychological science is needed to understand human behavior.[2]

In this chapter, the biblical counseling movement serves as the representation of biblical reductionism. This is because biblical reductionists are typically most interested in the intersection of psychology and theology within the realm of counseling. Few if any authors reflecting this view have addressed areas such as perception, social psychology, or other research areas in the field. Some within this movement acknowledge that psychological research can yield useful findings. For example, while being extremely dismissive of the role of psychology in counseling, movement leader Jay Adams states that "I do not wish to disregard science, but rather I welcome it as a useful adjunct for the purposes of illustrating, filling in generalizations with specifics, and challenging wrong human interpretations of scripture, thereby forcing the student to restudy the scriptures. However, in the area of psychiatry, science largely has given way to humanistic philosophy and gross speculation."[3] Yet this somewhat positive view of science does not translate into a full acceptance of scientific approaches for counseling or using science to understand patterns of human behavior.

Biblical Counseling

Biblical counselors believe that Scripture is sufficient for dealing with nonphysical "problems in living" and that in the realm of helping people with their problems, secular psychology has "usurped the work of the physician, but mostly the work of the preacher."[4] In other words, while secular psychology is embraced by the larger culture, it is unhelpful and even harmful in helping people with their problems.

The Association of Biblical Counselors describes biblical counseling this way:

> While Biblical counseling may exist as an event, it is most effective and best understood as a series of events; that is, as *a process*. The process

2. See Powlison, "Biblical Counseling View," 253–55.
3. Adams, *Competent to Counsel*, xxi.
4. Adams, "Big Umbrella," 8.

of encouraging sanctification, bearing with the suffering of others, and applying the truth of God's Word in a careful way takes time. It takes time to believe and follow the gospel more fully each day. The grace of God, the power of His Spirit, and faithful human effort are needed during the process. Therefore, for the counsel to be *Biblical* it must be rooted in God, exalting of Jesus Christ, enabled by the Holy Spirit, and offered in love.[5]

Adams's view of what biblical counseling should entail arose out of his dissatisfaction with the way psychiatry attempted to help people. David Powlison, in his historical overview of the biblical counseling movement, describes Adams as a "conscientiously biblicistic, local church pastor."[6] Adams believed that the primary provider of counseling for life's problems should be the pastor, not the professional psychologist. He believed that qualifications of a true counselor could "be summed up as extensive knowledge of the Scriptures, divine wisdom, and good will toward others."[7] He did not think specific training in the field of psychology or psychiatry was necessary, and, in fact, he believed that there was "no place in a biblical scheme for the psychiatrist as a separate practitioner."[8] Adams had consistent conflict not only with secular psychology but also with those who sought to integrate the findings of psychology with Christianity. He believed that Christianity didn't need psychology at all. Adams came to these conclusions in a couple of ways.

First, Adams believed that theories of psychology were inadequate for understanding and dealing with human problems. Adams began writing in the 1970s, and it is important to note that much of what he was criticizing were theories prevalent at that time, such as Freud's (psychoanalytic), Rogers's (humanistic), and Skinner's (behaviorist) theories, which—to varying degrees—went well beyond scientific findings or had philosophical implications. He argued that many of the presuppositions of those theories were antithetical to a Christian

---

5. Henderson, "Definition for Biblical Counseling."
6. Powlison, *Biblical Counseling Movement*, 28.
7. Adams, *Christian Counselor's Manual*, 13.
8. Adams, *Christian Counselor's Manual*, 9.

worldview.[9] Those presuppositions included naturalism and an underestimation of free will and personal responsibility. Furthermore, Adams noted that different theories of psychology contradicted each other. As a result, he concluded that there was no consensus in the field of psychology regarding either the methods or the goals for ideal mental health.[10]

Second, Adams believed that Scripture contained all that was necessary for assisting people with their problems. He referred to 2 Timothy 3:16–17: "All Scripture is God-breathed and is useful for teaching, rebuking, correcting and training in righteousness, so that the servant of God may be thoroughly equipped for every good work." He saw this verse as stating that Scripture was sufficient for equipping counselors to do the good work of helping those struggling with problems. The issue of the sufficiency of Scripture is one of the major themes of biblical counseling and will be examined more thoroughly later in this chapter. Adams's approach was not a scientific one, as he readily admitted in his early work, *Competent to Counsel*, writing, "The conclusions in this book are not based upon scientific findings. My method is presuppositional. I avowedly accept the inerrant Bible as the standard of all faith and practice. The Scriptures therefore are the basis and contain the criteria by which I have sought to make every judgment."[11]

Adams's counseling technique differed sharply from the client-centered Rogerian techniques that were popular at the time. In those techniques, counseling was often nondirective and clients guided their own goals and course through treatment. Adams, on the other hand, advocated for a direct approach that specifically guided people away from certain behaviors and toward others, with a heavy emphasis on repenting from sin. He referred to this as "putting off" the old sinful self and "putting on" the new, redeemed, Christian self.[12] While his approach focused on identifying sin as the cause of most problems in living, he was also quick to discuss God's grace and forgiveness.

9. Adams, *Christian Counselor's Manual*, 71–97.
10. Adams, "Big Umbrella," 24.
11. Adams, *Competent to Counsel*, xxi.
12. Adams, *Christian Counselor's Manual*, 177.

Others in the Christian community have agreed with Adams's assessment that secular psychology has nothing to offer the church and in fact should be seen as a threat to the church. Over thirty years after Adams started writing about counseling, John MacArthur, a popular preacher, wrote, "There may be no more serious threat to the life of the church today than the stampede to embrace the doctrines of secular psychology. They are a mass of human ideas that Satan has placed in the church as if they were powerful, life-changing truths from God."[13] Some Christian colleges and seminaries have developed biblical counseling programs.[14] In some cases, these programs have either replaced traditional psychology programs or been instituted in lieu of them. This is not to say that the biblical counseling approach is the dominant view within Christian higher education (it is not), but it does demonstrate that there is continued and growing interest in this approach.[15]

The Major Principles of Biblical Counseling

In examining the major principles of biblical counseling, two questions and their answers offered by biblical counselors stand out. One is the question, What are the causes of psychological disorders or, as many biblical counselors put it, "problems in living"? The second question is, Where do we find the solutions to these problems?

Sin—the Root Cause

Biblical counselors see sin as the major cause of psychological and behavioral problems. As Adams puts it, "There are, in the Scriptures, only three specified sources of personal problems in living: demonic activity (principally possession), personal sin, and organic illness. These three are interrelated. All options are covered under these heads,

13. MacArthur, "Rediscovering Biblical Counseling," 9.
14. Southern Baptist Theological Seminary and The Masters University and Seminary are examples of such institutions.
15. For example, the Association of Certified Biblical Counselors added more members in 2020 than in their first twenty-seven years combined. They have twenty-three hundred members and seventy-eight training centers. T. Johnson, "Ministry Update."

leaving no room for a fourth: non-organic mental illness."[16] Adams
believed that sin was at the heart of all nonorganic problems and that
to help people, a counselor needed to confront this sin. For example,
someone with anxiety might be seen as having that anxiety because of
sin in their life. This sin could involve sinful behaviors (e.g., stealing,
lying) or sinful motivations (e.g., desiring something like pleasure, ac-
colades, or material goods more than desiring God).[17] Or sin could be
present in the way they are dealing with a legitimate problem, such as
worrying about perfection and trying to obtain one's own righteousness
rather than trusting in the righteousness of Christ.

One of the major criticisms of Adams, even from within the biblical
counseling movement, is that he focused too much on personal sin.
While many biblical counselors agree that personal sin may be a cause
of many emotional and behavioral problems, they also agree that these
problems may be the result of being sinned against (e.g., abuse) or of
the general suffering that occurs in the brokenness of creation (e.g.,
coping with loss or illness).[18] This broader conceptualization of sin
(not just personal sin) allows for a more comprehensive view of how
sin impacts psychological functions. Nonetheless, biblical counseling
still tends to reduce most psychological problems to sinful actions or
spiritual struggles.

Many biblical counselors reject the notion that there is a legitimate category for nonorganic problems that are not spiritual in nature.
In his book *Blame It on the Brain?*, Edward Welch states, "Psychiat-
ric problems are always spiritual problems and sometimes physical
problems."[19] The concession that physical factors may impact mental
health is typically limited to physical conditions that are readily observable and measurable, like brain injuries or thyroid conditions. However,
many biblical counselors tend to be dismissive toward neurochemical explanations for disorders like depression and anxiety. They will
admit that there may be neurochemical differences that manifest in
the brain of someone with depression compared to someone without

16. Adams, *Christian Counselor's Manual*, 9.
17. Powlison, "Idols of the Heart and 'Vanity Fair.'"
18. See Lambert, *Biblical Counseling Movement after Adams*, 50–80.
19. Welch, *Blame It on the Brain?*, 106.

depression, but they caution that these differences may be the result of the depression and not the cause of it. Welch explains it this way: "Depression, disobedience, fatigue, dyslexia, and every other human behavior is represented on a neurochemical level. This doesn't mean that the brain causes all these behaviors, but that the brain expresses differences in behavior at a chemical level."[20] So, in their view it isn't clear if depression causes low levels of the neurotransmitter serotonin or if low levels of serotonin cause depression.

Biblical counselors are often concerned that secular views of psychological problems may explain away or justify sinful behaviors. Adams felt that terms like "emotional problems" and "mental illness" were euphemisms that masked the role of sin in people's problems.[21] Therefore, biblical counselors place little confidence in professional diagnoses found in the DSM-5.[22] An example of the biblical counseling approach can be seen in the book *Counseling the Hard Cases*, edited by Stuart Scott and Heath Lambert. This book provides case studies of problems the DSM-5 would classify (e.g., postpartum depression, bipolar disorder, obsessive-compulsive disorder) and reframes them and their treatment through the lens of biblical counseling. One of these cases involves a woman named Mary and her crippling fear of somehow contracting HIV/AIDS. The biblical counselor involved in this case frames Mary's problems as being ultimately about sin, stating, "Mary was experiencing the mental and physical consequences of her sinful failure to trust God."[23] The treatment involved helping Mary trust in Christ and reminding her to take rest in Christ from her fears.

Sufficiency of Scripture—the Cure for Problems in Living

Since sin is seen as the root problem and ultimate cause of psychological issues, the solution to these problems in living resides in Scripture. This is often referred to as the "sufficiency of Scripture"[24]

---

20. Welch, *Blame It on the Brain?*, 110.

21. See Adams, *Christian Counselor's Manual*, 109–11.

22. *The Diagnostic and Statistics Manual of Mental Disorders*, 5th ed. (*DSM-5*) is the major diagnostic tool used in clinical psychology.

23. Wicket, "'Mary' and Paralyzing Fear," 123.

24. See Lambert, *Theology of Biblical Counseling*, specifically chap. 2.

and is the second major tenet of biblical counseling. As Wayne Mack puts it, "Scripture should be the sum and substance of our counseling instruction, because it deals with *all* the issues of life that are necessary for us to understand."[25] Biblical counselors believe that Scripture itself claims to be sufficient for dealing with life's problems. This is commonly supported by pointing to verses such as Romans 15:14, 2 Timothy 3:16–17, and 2 Peter 1:3.[26] Whether the sin is personal sin, the sin of others, or the general brokenness of creation, the ultimate solution is the same—namely, Jesus Christ. While this view causes some critics to assume that biblical counselors apply solutions simplistically (e.g., "Trust in Jesus and your problems will go away"), most biblical counselors believe the goal is to gradually increase the client's sanctification (i.e., greater holiness) and apply the work of Christ to their current situation.

Biblical counselors do not necessarily see the Bible as a textbook that addresses every psychological problem, but they do believe the Bible and its themes are sufficient for dealing with every psychological problem. So, while the Bible doesn't specifically address generalized anxiety disorder, it does speak about worry and trusting God.[27] The Bible doesn't discuss major depressive disorder, but it does guide us to rejoice and have joy even in difficult circumstances.[28] Some biblical counselors will grant that secular sources may illustrate, illuminate, and deepen our understanding, but they are not necessary.[29] In other words, one can counsel with Scripture alone, but one cannot counsel properly with secular psychology alone.

---

25. Mack, "Providing Instruction through Biblical Counseling," 163.

26. Romans 15:14: "I myself am convinced, my brothers and sisters, that you yourselves are full of goodness, filled with knowledge and competent to instruct one another"; 2 Tim. 3:16–17: "All Scripture is God-breathed and is useful for teaching, rebuking, correcting and training in righteousness, so that the servant of God may be thoroughly equipped for every good work"; 2 Peter 1:3: "His divine power has given us everything we need for a godly life through our knowledge of him who called us by his own glory and goodness."

27. E.g., Isa. 12:2: "Surely God is my salvation; I will trust and not be afraid. The LORD, the LORD himself, is my strength and my defense; he has become my salvation."

28. E.g., 1 Thess. 5:16–18: "Rejoice always, pray continually, give thanks in all circumstances; for this is God's will for you in Christ Jesus."

29. See Lambert, *Biblical Counseling Movement after Adams*, 49–80.

Some in this movement see no value in mainstream psychology. In dismissing the value of secular approaches to problems, John Mac-Arthur writes, "Human therapies are embraced most eagerly by the spiritually weak, those who are shallow or ignorant of biblical truth and who are unwilling to accept the path of suffering that leads to spiritual maturity and deeper communion with God. The unfortunate effect is that these people remain immature, held back by a self-imposed dependence on some pseudo-Christian method or psycho-quackery that actually stifles real growth."[30]

Because of its focus on Scripture as the solution, biblical counseling is seen as being most applicable to professing Christians. What about those who do not believe in Christianity? Biblical counselors answer that the first step is to evangelize these unbelievers and get them to trust in Christ to open the door to the resources that Scripture provides. After discussing the need for repentance and confession in counseling, Heath Lambert states, "Biblical counselors understand that the only people who confess their sins are those whose hearts have been changed by the Holy Spirit. This does not mean that we cannot have counseling conversations with people who are not converted. It means that such counseling will always be decidedly evangelistic."[31]

Worldview Foundations for Biblical Reductionism

Before providing an evaluation of biblical reductionism, it is important to examine the religious and philosophical foundations for such an approach. As described in chapter 4, Christians who might characterize themselves as fundamentalists will tend toward a position described by theologian H. Richard Niebuhr as "Christ against culture." This fundamentalist view appears to align with a biblical reductionist approach. To paraphrase theologian Herman Bavinck, this approach tends to rescue and snatch ideas out of the world, which lies in wickedness. Hence the tendency for biblical counselors to accept only small portions of secular psychology. In addition, this fundamentalist approach

---

30. MacArthur, "Rediscovering Biblical Counseling," 14.
31. Lambert, *Theology of Biblical Counseling*, 230.

tends to align with a more literal interpretation of Scripture and places scriptural truths well above scientific truths. Biblical counselors may not reject all science (particularly natural science), but they do pick and choose scientific findings that align easily with biblical narratives.

Theologically, this view aligns with a strong emphasis on the work of the Holy Spirit; a strong view of personal agency, sin, and responsibility; and a strong support of body-soul dualism. This last emphasis helps to account for concerns about secular psychology. Dualism suggests that most of the essential mental activities (e.g., morality, ethics, personal responsibility, understanding of God) reside in an ethereal (i.e., nonmaterial) mind-soul. Since the soul is not amenable to observation or scientific manipulation, the notion of psychological science (i.e., science of the soul) seems untenable or even dangerous. Therefore, the proper approach is to engage in spiritual change rather than behavioral change.

One other aspect to note about biblical reductionism is the fact that it grew out of a reaction to nonbiblical worldview perspectives that were prevalent in therapy during the second half of the twentieth century. As described in chapter 3, approaches such as psychoanalysis, humanistic psychology, and applied behaviorism included many nonscientific assumptions that ran counter to biblical perspectives. While many of these assumptions can still be found in several psychological theories and practices, many of these positions have softened by, for example, placing greater emphasis on personal responsibility, placing less emphasis on deterministic factors, and respecting the moral and ethical positions of clients. As discussed in chapter 3, the changing landscape of psychological research, theory, and practice means that attempts to integrate faith and psychology require regular updates.

An Evaluation of Biblical Reductionism

From a Christian perspective, one of the positive aspects of biblical reductionism is the high value afforded to Scripture. This approach tends to affirm common Christian views of ontology, teleology, and axiology. Biblical reductionists do not limit the application of Scripture to one specific sphere of life. Theologians from the reformed tradition (see chap. 4) have written about how the Bible and theology should impact all areas of one's life, which biblical counselors contend they do.[32] Relatedly, most Christians would agree that Scripture speaks to many of the problems and issues that can impact our lives. Scripture provides rich resources for issues such as interpersonal relations, conflict resolution, forgiveness, living out one's values, and emotions such as fear, anxiety, joy, and hope. Many would agree that biblical counselors are correct that we should heed and embrace the wisdom found in the Bible, even though they may disagree with the idea that Scripture is wholly sufficient for dealing with all problems in living.

Many agree with some of the criticisms leveled at various forms of psychology. This began with Adams's critique of Freud, Skinner, and Rogers and continues today.[33] As mentioned earlier, several psychological theories contain presuppositions that can be seen as running counter to a Christian worldview, and this approach has correctly identified several of these worldview assumptions. Furthermore, biblical counselors have rightly raised the question as to what ideal mental health should look like. The proper goal, outcome, or telos is of vital importance, and biblical counseling has pointed out that Scripture helps answer these types of questions and should be a valuable resource for framing a Christian view of mental health. Additionally, much has been written about the over-psychologizing of society and how some issues that were once seen as normal variations in thought and behavior are now seen as pathologies.[34] Biblical counselors echo some secular sentiment concerning these issues and offer another point of view on our understanding of mental health.

Relatedly, biblical counselors have pointed to instances in which the larger culture uncritically accepted psychological claims that later turned out to be questionable. A good example can be seen in the issue of self-esteem. In the 1970s and 1980s, several self-esteem programs were put in place in many schools. These programs were premised on

---

32. As Abraham Kuyper puts it, "There is not a square inch in the whole domain of human existence over which Christ, who is Sovereign over all, does not cry 'Mine'!" Kuyper, *Abraham Kuyper*, 488.

33. Adams, *Christian Counselor's Manual*, 71–97.

34. See Wakefield, "Diagnostic Issues and Controversies in *DSM-5*."

the idea that higher levels of self-esteem should lead to better outcomes (e.g., higher grades, better behavior). Some of these programs were based on ideas championed by secular psychologists at the time.[35] Yet research and experience have shown that the benefits of such programs are, at best, overstated, and in some cases, the programs may have had negative effects on learning.[36] Despite these findings and a shift in how the scientific community views self-esteem, many self-esteem programs persist, and the view that many social problems are due to low self-esteem is still influential. So, even though the scientific view has changed, the original, uncritical acceptance of the premise that self-esteem is paramount echoes through American culture to this day. However, some writers coming from a biblical perspective have consistently questioned the focus on self-esteem and, in retrospect, seem somewhat prophetic.[37] There may be times when the biblical reductionist perspective can serve as a voice in the wilderness, drawing attention to faulty assumptions and claims in mainstream psychology.

On the critical side, other Christian psychologists have raised several shortcomings and weaknesses of the biblical reductionist view. One criticism is that biblical reductionists may oversimplify the role of sin as the cause of psychological problems.[38] While many Christians may agree that many problems (psychological or otherwise) are a result of the general brokenness of creation that occurred because of the fall, it may be overly simplistic to reduce most problems to sin issues. While current biblical counselors acknowledge that problems in life may occur due to the sin of others or general suffering, they still tend to focus on personal responsibility for one's problems.[39] They recognize that we are broken, but the focus is on individual sin rather than the collective and structural nature of brokenness. They point out that even though a person may suffer from the sins of others (e.g., abuse, neglect), it is still that person's responsibility how they respond.

---

35. For a review, see Ward, "Filling the World with Self-esteem."
36. Baumeister and Vohs, "Revisiting Our Reappraisal."
37. Vitz, *Psychology as Religion*, 15–19.
38. E. Johnson, *God and Soul Care*, 278–98; and McRay, Yarhouse, and Butman, *Modern Psychopathologies*, 90.
39. See Lambert, *Biblical Counseling Movement after Adams*, 57–66.

This places a great deal of responsibility for one's problems on the self. So while they understand the role of responsible agency, biblical reductionists may underestimate the limitations brought about by social circumstances, genetics, neurotransmitters, strong mental habits, unconscious thoughts, and so on.

Related to this, biblical reductionists seem to minimize embodiment—especially the idea that our mental operations arise from our bodily existence. Despite the considerable body of research demonstrating the vital role that neurotransmitters play in the etiology of psychological disorders, many biblical counselors are skeptical of viewing neurotransmitters as a causal factor. Contemporary research also stresses the multifaceted nature of psychological problems. For example, the biopsychosocial model of psychology posits that psychological problems are often the result of various biological, cognitive, and environmental factors interacting with one another.[40] By reducing problems to just the category of sin, many biblical reductionists overlook these nuances, and as a result, a true understanding of the problems may be obscured.

Another shortcoming that has been raised is that biblical reductionists tend to focus more on counseling than on scientific research and in some ways are dealing with an outdated view of psychology. At one point, dismissing Freud, Rogers, and others made sense in part because their approaches were more widely accepted in the field of psychology, and it made sense to engage with and debate against these perspectives. Yet as these approaches have become less dominant and as clinical psychology becomes more focused on research-based approaches, engaging with current psychological research in clinical areas seems increasingly important. For example, MacArthur complains about society's focus on self-esteem and criticizes psychology for promoting it, but as discussed above, scientific psychology agrees with much of his assessment.[41] Scientific psychology has demonstrated the shortcomings of the self-esteem movement and could be seen as an ally in some sense, but biblical counselors often seem unwilling to fully engage with the field.

40. See Porter, "Biopsychosocial Model in Mental Health."
41. MacArthur, "Counseling and the Sinfulness of Humanity."

The sufficiency question also raises important issues. Biblical reductionists see Scripture as sufficient to understand and solve psychological problems, but several Christian scholars disagree.[42] These critics agree that Scripture can play a vital role in dealing with psychological problems and in understanding human nature, but they also value contributions from other areas, including psychology. They see the topic through the lens of common grace, the idea that God allows even unbelievers to uncover and understand part of his creation. So, if psychology can assist in our understanding of obsessive-compulsive disorder or conflict resolution, it ought to be embraced. Biblical reductionists disagree with this and view secular psychology as something that can be supplemental at best. Their view is often that anything good found in secular systems of counseling can already be found in the Bible.

Related to the sufficiency issue, the biblical reductionist stance that Scripture itself claims it is sufficient for all problems of living is based on certain verses that can be interpreted in different ways. For example, biblical counselors use 2 Peter 1:3, which states, "His divine power has given us *everything we need* for a godly life through our knowledge of him who called us by his own glory and goodness" to demonstrate that the Bible provides everything we need for our lives. Yet this verse could be read as talking about everything we need for salvation and not necessarily everything we need for all aspects of living. Eric Johnson suggests that Scripture contains claims that it is sufficient for salvation, faith, and practice (salvific doctrinal sufficiency) but that it is an error to broaden this view of sufficiency to include all psychological problems.[43]

It is even questionable whether biblical reductionists themselves rely on Scripture alone when formulating their treatments. J. Cameron Fraser and David Powlison both point out that Adams was heavily impacted by the psychological viewpoints of O. Hobart Mowrer, an influential behavioral psychologist who emphasized the personal responsibility of the counselee as an important factor in understanding and

---

42. Jones, "Integration Response to Biblical Counseling," 278–79; and Vanhoozer, "Sufficiency of Scripture," 231–32.

43. E. Johnson, *Foundations for Soul Care*, 177–93.

dealing with problems.[44] Yet Mowrer did not operate from Scripture or even from a Christian perspective. This acceptance of Mowrer seems to contradict the idea that counseling should be guided by Scripture alone. It seems that when biblical counselors find something they agree with in secular techniques, they tend to say that the Bible taught that first, and therefore secular psychology was not needed. An example of this can be seen in one biblical counselor's approach to dealing with a client with anorexia. While couched in Christian language, part of the treatment involved the client monitoring her thoughts and thinking of ways to replace negative thoughts with more beneficial ones.[45] This resembles standard cognitive therapy that many secular psychologists would use. It is difficult to see how the biblical counselor would have generated this technique from a "plain reading" of Bible verses. They may point to a verse about taking every thought captive to Christ (2 Cor. 10:5) as the grounds for this approach,[46] but while that verse certainly fits this approach, would they have come to this application without something like cognitive-behavioral therapy (CBT)? It can seem like biblical counselors are finding something effective and then searching for a proof text that supports the approach.

To be clear, many Christian psychologists agree that the Bible and theology offer tools to help with problems. Christianity has a wealth of tools to help us understand and bear suffering, to help us find purpose and meaning, and to help guide our behavior. The Bible tells us how to deal with anxiety, but is there a difference between normal anxiety and generalized anxiety disorder (GAD)? Telling someone with obsessive-compulsive disorder (OCD) that they just need to trust or rest in the Lord may not be helpful if the problem isn't one of motivation or rational thought. Biblical counselors may oversimplify a problem to claim that the Bible has the answer for it. One can see how the idea of trusting God would be useful in helping people reframe things in CBT, but CBT also offers other tools that might be helpful even if there is not a direct reference to religion. It seems possible (or

44. Fraser, *Developments in Biblical Counseling,* 51; and Powlison, *Biblical Counseling Movement,* 185.

45. Peace, "'Ashley' and Anorexia."

46. Lambert, *Theology of Biblical Counseling,* 22.

even likely) that something like GAD or OCD is due not to a lack of faith but to neurochemical activity or a distorted way of thinking. Therefore, secular psychology may have vital contributions for how to combat these problems.

In short, many Christian psychologists do not believe that every psychological issue has its roots in a spiritual issue. This conflation of psychological issues and spiritual issues can create confusion. While there is certainly a degree of overlap between these two domains (our spirituality influences our psychology and vice versa), the distinction seems important. Secular psychology doesn't lead to salvation of course, but it helps deal with some proximate issues that may interfere with daily living. Fixing a broken leg doesn't directly help with salvation, but doctors still serve a vital purpose. Could psychologists and psychiatrists be viewed the same way? It seems that one could affirm that knowing about a loving, powerful, gracious God would be helpful for someone struggling with anxiety and that this would also serve the ultimate purpose of salvation, but does that mean that any and all help for anxiety needs to have a reference to God? Can we help someone with crippling anxiety who doesn't believe in God the same way we could treat a broken arm of someone who doesn't believe in God? Can't we treat the anxiety in one context and move toward the gospel in the other? Is this still being faithful? These are questions that biblical reductionists need to wrestle with.

QUESTIONS FOR DISCUSSION

1. How does your own experience in religious settings compare to the biblical reductionist approach? Have you encountered support of or skepticism toward psychology within church settings?

2. Biblical reductionists argue that Scripture is sufficient to understand human nature, and that it is the real remedy for problems that clinical and counseling psychology have addressed. How would you respond? Can you give evidence for the Bible's sufficiency or insufficiency in these regards?

3. The argument of some biblical reductionists is that holiness (biblical obedience) and mental health should be clearly related to each other. What are your reasons for agreeing or disagreeing with this statement?

7

Complementary Models

If you have ever watched professional artists work with acrylic paints, you know they are expert at mixing and matching paint colors. First, they know which colors can coexist even though they don't match. They know which colors complement each other. Finally, they know how to mix two colors together to make a new color. A complementary framework for relating faith to psychology encompasses three slightly different versions that are analogous to the three ways painters work with color. In this chapter we discuss three complementary models, recognizing that this is not necessarily an exhaustive list and that these models exist on a continuum. We also want to stress that these models have more commonalities than differences. For example, all three models affirm the following:

1. Psychology and theology are useful tools for examining human nature and behavior.
2. Psychology and theology cannot be reduced to the other (i.e., explaining one discipline using the ideas from the other), which is what the scientific and biblical reductionist approaches assert.
3. Psychology should be viewed as a science and should use the scientific method. Psychological science does not need to be

transformed into something else (i.e., using a very different method to gain knowledge), which is what the humanizing approach described in the next chapter asserts.

4. Insights from both psychology and theology together provide a fuller, more complete picture of human nature than either area alone.

While all the complementary forms take psychology and Christianity seriously, each subsequent level offers more direct interaction between Christianity and psychology.

To compare these models, we start each section by examining how the model can be used in the study of interpersonal forgiveness. We have chosen this topic because forgiveness is an area of interest in both psychology and theology. While the links between forgiveness and Christian theology are likely clear, forgiveness has also received increasing attention in psychology. Researchers are interested in what causes someone to grant and seek forgiveness and what the outcomes are related to forgiveness. Interpersonal forgiveness has been examined from a variety of perspectives and linked with mental and physical health benefits.[1] So how might a researcher combine the theological approach with the psychological approach to address interpersonal forgiveness?

Territorialism

Imagine a theologian with a great deal of interest in why people should forgive one another. She believes that forgiveness is ultimately a spiritual issue, and while psychology may be useful for studying certain aspects of human nature, theology is uniquely suited for a spiritual topic like forgiveness. She views the work of psychology on forgiveness a bit skeptically since she doesn't think it is the proper tool to understand forgiveness.

This approach represents a type of integration that occurs when theology and psychology are restricted to specific areas of inquiry—like

---

1. Rasmussen et al., "Meta-Analytic Connections between Forgiveness and Health."

a painter identifying colors that can coexist even though they don't match. Some call this approach territorialism[2] or a parallels model.[3] In this approach, psychology and theology are used to study different aspects of human nature and have little direct impact on each other. For example, psychology would be used to study things like memory, depression, learning, and brain processes because these topics are amenable to empirical study. On the other hand, theology would be used to explore topics like morality, ethics, the afterlife, and sanctification. The key idea here is that different topics are assigned to different disciplines, and therefore what psychology is studying about human nature is seen as separate from what theology is studying. Proponents of the territorialist approach may agree with biologist Stephen Jay Gould's "nonoverlapping magisteria" principle. Gould believed that there should be no conflicts between religion and science "because each subject has a legitimate magisterium, or domain of teaching authority—and these magisteria do not overlap."[4] One realm is not necessarily more or less important than the other. Rather, each realm has a different purpose and set of evaluative tools.

This territorialist approach is illustrated in therapy practiced by Clinton McLemore, a Christian clinical psychologist who describes his interactions with a client named Robert.[5] Robert was seeing McLemore for help with his inability to form romantic relationships. While therapy was helping Robert, something outside therapy had the largest impact. Robert appeared to be more confident and willing to pursue new relationships after he engaged in a sexual encounter with a new acquaintance. McLemore was conflicted about this positive outcome because he knew that Robert's sexual encounter outside of marriage was viewed as immoral from a Christian worldview. So how should he respond to Robert's situation? McLemore notes that Robert expressed no interest in Christianity, and he feels that Robert would not have responded well to a discussion of Christian sexual ethics. Therefore, McLemore writes, "The Christian psychotherapist

2. Evans, *Preserving the Person*, 102.
3. Carter and Narramore, *Integration of Psychology and Theology*, 91–92.
4. Gould, "Nonoverlapping Magisteria," 16.
5. McLemore, *Scandal of Psychotherapy*, 69–72.

does sometimes have to choose between supporting what is good, in the sense that it will help their client emotionally, and what is good in the sense that it conforms to the Christian ideal."[6] For McLemore, Robert's emotional/mental health was a separate issue from his spiritual health, and while he would certainly not personally recommend Robert's behavior, he did not see it as his place to critique the behavior in the therapy context. For McLemore, both theology and psychology are important, but they are restricted to their respective territories. Therefore, when a person is operating as a clinician, psychology informs their actions, but in their personal life and moral decision making, Christianity holds sway. This same principle would apply to psychological science. A scientist must set aside religious questions and operate primarily by the rules of science when investigating the causes of human behavior.

Perspectivalism

Another potential approach to a topic like forgiveness is to use both psychology and theology to examine the topic but to have each area focus on different aspects of forgiveness. Psychology could examine forgiveness in terms of its benefits, what makes forgiveness more or less likely, and what emotions are related to forgiveness granting and forgiveness seeking. Theology would be concerned with why we should seek and grant forgiveness and how we are motivated to forgive because God has forgiven us. In other words, science would examine the mechanisms of forgiveness, while theology would examine the value and meaning of forgiveness—like two colors that complement each other.

This version of complementary integration, sometimes referred to as perspectivalism[7] or the levels-of-explanation view,[8] differs slightly from the territorialist approach in that greater effort is made to show the connection between psychological science and theology. According to perspectivalism, both psychology and theology can be applied to

6. McLemore, *Scandal of Psychotherapy*, 73.
7. Evans, *Preserving the Person*, 105–6.
8. Myers, "Levels-of-Explanation View," 51.

almost any topic, but each operates according to a different perspective. The term *levels of explanation* suggests that theology and psychology may legitimately address similar issues, but each operates at a different level of analysis. David Myers, a social psychologist, and Malcolm Jeeves, a neuropsychologist, are two Christian psychologists who have written extensively about this approach. The analogies they use to explain perspectivalism are that of a painting and a phone message: "To say the painting is 'nothing but' or 'reducible to' blobs of paint may at one level be true, but it misses the beauty and meaning that can be seen if one steps back and views the painting as a whole. To consider a phone caller's voice as reducible to electrical impulses on the phone line is extremely useful for some scientific purposes. But if you view it as nothing more you will miss its message."[9]

Therefore, a perspectivalist sees each explanation as separate but also incomplete without the other account. The perspectivalist is more willing than the territorialist to show continuity between scientific and religious explanations of reality. For example, while a strict territorialist might state that forgiveness is a theological topic and should only be studied using theology, a perspectivalist would agree that the two ways of knowing (i.e., scientific and religious) are separate, but they would also see them as complementing and completing each other. Since each perspective or level is limited, a complete picture of an issue like forgiveness is provided only when both perspectives are applied. As mentioned above, psychology would be viewed as appropriate and effective for studying certain aspects of forgiveness (e.g., the antecedents and outcomes of forgiveness), while theology would be appropriate for other aspects (e.g., why someone should forgive and/or seek forgiveness). Then the two perspectives could be brought together to provide a more complete picture. Similarly, psychology would be able to study religion by looking at how people come to believe and the behavioral outcomes of belief, while theology would focus on the content and doctrine of a religion. In this way, perspectivalism avoids the problems of territorialism by being able to address topics that may be relevant to multiple fields of inquiry.

9. Myers and Jeeves, *Psychology through the Eyes of Faith*, 8.

The key idea is that no one perspective or level is sufficient to fully explain a phenomenon. Nor is one level used to explain away another level. We need all the levels to gain a complete understanding of a topic. Using a different example and including additional levels of understanding, we can see that the topic of aggression can be looked at from different perspectives. Biology could examine the areas of the brain that are activated during aggression or the impact of testosterone on aggressive tendencies. Psychology could examine situational influences on aggression (e.g., aversive stimuli, observational learning). Sociology could look at group-level phenomena like cultural expressions of aggression and violent crime rates, while philosophy could look at how we think about the meaning or impact of aggression. Finally, theology could examine if and when aggression might be justifiable in the eyes of God (e.g., just war theory, pacifism). Understanding aggression completely would require multiple disciplines and multiple epistemologies.

Perspectivalists acknowledge that values and beliefs can influence how one conducts and understands research. In this way, they have a more postpositivist view of science. Jeeves acknowledges that worldview can shape our interpretations when he writes, "Our presuppositions not only influence the interpretation of our scientific data; they also, at times powerfully, influence the interpretations we impose on the 'data of Scripture.' In that sense all our ideas are vulnerable to error and bias."[10] However, perspectivalists believe that once these biases are acknowledged, one should try to remove them as much as possible. As Myers puts it, "Being mindful of hidden values within psychological science should motivate us to clean the cloudy spectacles through which we view the world."[11] In other words, even though true objectivity is impossible, one should still strive for it when theorizing and interpreting psychological data.

In practice, then, a Christian psychological researcher using the perspectivalist approach may use theology to help direct their application of research, but the actual hypotheses and interpretations in

---

10. Jeeves, *Human Nature at the Millennium*, 238.
11. Myers, "Levels-of-Explanation View," 54.

the realm of science should be similar to those of a secular scientist. Jeeves states, "While in other areas of science personal values certainly influence such things as which problems we choose to study, which methods we will use, and if, how, when, and where any results will be applied, nevertheless the values do not intrude into science per se."[12] Perspectivalists attempt to remain as objective as possible when doing the actual work of psychological science. This differs from the next approach, integrationism, in which Christian values and presuppositions are seen as enhancing all aspects of psychological research.

Integrationism

In this final approach to studying forgiveness, a researcher might agree with perspectivalists in many ways but might extend the reach of theology by using it to create new hypotheses or alternative interpretations of research findings—new colors. For example, Scripture does not speak that much about the concept of self-forgiveness, while the field of psychology has many studies on the topic. This might lead an integrationist to be skeptical of the utility of self-forgiveness. Might a propensity to forgive oneself decrease the motivation to seek forgiveness from others or from God? If so, then any short-term benefits of self-forgiveness might be suspect from a Christian point of view. Of course, this would then have to be tested, perhaps by looking at the relationship between self-forgiveness and forgiveness seeking. It remains an empirical question that can be assessed by psychological science, but the prediction and interpretations would be led by theology. Alternatively, if research showed positive long-term benefits of self-forgiveness and no deficits in seeking forgiveness, then this might allow self-forgiveness to become incorporated into theological views of forgiveness.

This approach, in which there is greater interaction between theology and psychology, is referred to as integrationism.[13] While the territorialist approach places a strict wall between the two areas and the

---

12. Jeeves, *Human Nature at the Millennium*, 146.
13. E. Johnson, *Psychology and Christianity*, 34–35.

perspectivalist approach maintains the distinctiveness of each area, the integrationist approach stresses ways in which theology might inform or shape psychological theory and practice. Both integrationists and perspectivalists agree with the postpositivist view that true, value-free objectivity is not actually possible, but they differ in how they react to this. While perspectivalists attempt to be as objective as possible and do not want theology to have a direct influence on psychological science, integrationists believe that since objectivity is impossible, it is better to embrace one's worldview values when conducting science. Values and judgments influence all aspects of science, and therefore an explicit acknowledgment of that influence is preferable to pretending it is not there. In this way, Christian values and beliefs can and should have more of a direct impact on psychological science than is recognized under the perspectivalist approach.

How might Christian values impact the way one conducts science under this model? The empirical methodology of integrationists would not differ from that of a perspectivalist or even a secular scientist. They would conduct studies in much the same way. However, their worldview could affect their science in the following ways:

1. Their motivations for research: A Christian worldview may raise certain topics (e.g., forgiveness, altruism) that motivate researchers to examine them empirically.

2. The formation of hypotheses: A Christian worldview would impact the predictions that one makes. For example, a Christian researcher might expect to see a positive relationship between certain types of suffering and the virtue of perseverance.

3. The interpretation of data: All data is theory laden, and therefore a Christian worldview would be used to understand what the data points to, which interpretations might be favored, and how the evidence comports with Scripture.

4. The application of research findings: Once knowledge is gained, it should be used for the glory of God. So, knowledge of how to increase forgiveness could be used to develop reconciliation programs.

Perspectivalists would likely agree with principles 1 and 4 but might be wary of 2 and 3. Perspectivalists are fine with theology playing a role in shaping topics of study and applications, but they are concerned with theology being involved in theory formation and data interpretation.

Stanton Jones is a good representative of the integrationist viewpoint. He argues that theology should be able to speak directly to science because everyone brings their worldview to their scientific process. He points out that theories do not simply arise from a set of simple facts. Rather, worldviews and presuppositions guide our understanding of the facts. Jones does believe that predictions derived from presuppositions still need to be tested and that, if appropriate, presuppositions may need to be refined based on observation.[14] Therefore, Christians should be up front about how a Christian worldview and presuppositions are influencing their formation of hypotheses and interpretations of data. As Jones puts it,

> The explicit incorporation of values and worldviews into the scientific process will not necessarily result in a loss of objectivity or methodological rigor. What is new about this proposal is not the incorporation of assumptions into the process, but rather the proposal that psychological scientists and practitioners be more explicit about the interaction of religious belief and psychology. If scientists, especially psychologists, are operating out of worldview assumptions that include the religious, and if the influence of such factors is actually inevitable, then the advancement of the scientific enterprise would be facilitated by making those beliefs explicitly available for public inspection and discourse.[15]

In addition, some who use this approach have argued that true integration of Christianity and psychology must involve an understanding of our telos, or ultimate goal.[16] Secular psychology has the goal of human flourishing, but removed from a theological understanding of human nature, it struggles to define what the ideal view of human

14. Jones, "Constructive Relationship," 186–88.
15. Jones, "Constructive Relationship," 193.
16. Murphy, "Constructing a Radical-Reformation Research Program in Psychology," 55–56.

nature is. By using Christian theology and the inherent teleology contained within it, a person can begin to create a view of what human flourishing is and how to obtain it. The answers to these types of questions can then shape research programs and applications. In this way, a Christian is not "doing psychology" just like a secular scientist, even if they are using similar empirical methodology. One example is the Christian ideal of self-renunciation (i.e., a willingness to give up one's own wishes or desires) and how it would contrast with contemporary psychology's focus on self-fulfillment.[17]

Under some integrationist approaches, theology may be given higher priority over science. This is not an ignoring of science (as one might see under biblical reductionism), but when theology and psychological science appear to conflict, integrationists tend to defer to theology. As Jones puts it, "Integration of Christianity and psychology is our living out—in this particular area—of the lordship of Christ over all of existence by our giving his special revelation—God's true Word—its appropriate place of authority in determining our fundamental beliefs about and practices toward all of reality and toward our academic subject matter in particular."[18] This integrationist approach does not seek to redefine science, but it does put science under the authority of Scripture. Everett Worthington, a clinical psychologist, appears to agree with this deference to theology when he writes, "I believe that we must clearly adhere to faith rather than science if they were ever to come into serious conflict."[19] Yet he thinks such conflicts are unlikely and may stem from a misunderstanding of either theology or science. He points out that we are dealing with interpretations of Scripture and not exactly Scripture itself.

In many situations the difference between an integrationist and a perspectivalist will be minimal. For example, when studying functions of neurotransmitters like dopamine or serotonin, it is unlikely that an integrationist's Christian worldview will have much direct impact on their science. Or when studying the psychology of memory, both a perspectivalist and an integrationist would likely agree that a Christian

17. Murphy, "Theological Resources for Integration," 42–52.
18. Jones, "Integration View," 102.
19. Worthington, *Coming to Peace with Psychology*, 115.

worldview might dictate what ideas and information should be put into memory, but the study of the mechanisms of memory (the realm of psychology) would be minimally impacted by this worldview. Differences between these approaches become more apparent for issues with greater overlap between theology and psychology. Issues such as forgiveness, emotions, prosocial behavior, mental well-being, personality, sexuality, and therapy are examples of areas where an integrationist would allow their worldview to speak more directly to how they would conduct their science because these areas are more dependent on presuppositions about human nature.

So, an integrationist might use Scripture's discussion on the fruit of the Spirit (Gal. 5:22–23) to make predictions about what individual characteristics might be associated with one's religiosity. An integrationist might also use the concept of being made in the image of God to speak to what we should expect and strive toward for human flourishing. For example, this is one way that the image of God has been understood: because God is relational as the Trinity (i.e., three persons—Father, Son, and Holy Spirit—in one), humans have been created to be relational.[20] Based on this theology, an integrationist would favor studying personality by looking at relationships and interrelatedness rather than independence and uniqueness. Similarly, therapeutic techniques could be evaluated through a Christian lens. Jones and Butman have examined various approaches to therapy, showing places of agreement and disagreement with a Christian worldview.[21] These are just some of the ways an integrationist might bring their worldview to bear on all aspects of science and application.

Under the integrationist framework, theology may take the lead, but that doesn't mean the relationship with science is one-way. This is a two-way conversation. Theology helps shape scientific endeavors, but scientific discoveries can also impact theology. If psychological data continually challenges a traditional theological stance, then that stance should be reexamined in light of the findings. After criticizing the way psychology has been used to dismiss or reinterpret theology,

20. Barth, *Church Dogmatics*, vol. III/1, 197–98.
21. See Jones and Butman, *Modern Psychotherapies*.

Jones states, "These roles should not be simply reversed, with religion dictating to the science of psychology (or any science). The relationship between the two must be dialogical. . . . New findings in cosmology, sociobiology, philosophy, anthropology, sociology, and even psychology should infuse and affect the religious enterprise. Just as changing from a geocentric to heliocentric version of existence had a number of effects on religious belief, as have other scientific discoveries and revolutions, so also must religion be prepared to change as it engages in a constructive dialogue with psychology."[22] Therefore, theology does not become a mere filter, and all scientific findings do not need to be made to fit into a specific theological stance. Empirical evidence can be used to revisit theological stances. However, this is done cautiously since one's Christian presuppositions should be the guiding principle. An *initial* default may be to defer to theology in cases of conflict.

Worldview Foundations for the Three Complementary Models

The three complementary models have similar views concerning all but one of the significant philosophical positions (i.e., cosmology, ontology, teleology, anthropology, and axiology). For example, in terms of anthropology (nature of humans), the similarities would be far greater than any differences, with most adherents accepting basic tenets such as "humans are responsible but limited agents," "humans are embodied but also directed toward spiritual concerns," and so on.

The primary philosophical difference between these positions is their view of epistemology (nature of knowledge). As described earlier, all three positions value scientific findings, but they also value religion as a valid source of truth. However, the territorialist position leans toward a positivist view—confined to scientific endeavors alone—while the other two tend toward a more postpositivist direction (i.e., there is an objective truth, but it cannot be known perfectly). For the perspectivalist, objective scientific understanding may not be perfectly obtainable, but it is still a goal for which we should strive. For inte-

---

22. Jones, "Constructive Relationship," 195.

grationists, presuppositions that Christians hold to be "self-evident" should shape and guide scientific inquiry—especially for human behavior. This position would lie somewhere between postpositivism and constructivism-interpretivism. It would not be completely interpretive because there is an assumption that an objective truth exists. However, they would also agree with the philosopher Kant, who suggested (see chap. 1) that "human claims about nature cannot be independent of inside-the-head processes of the knowing subject."[23] For the integrationist, these inside-the-head processes of knowing should be driven by a scriptural worldview.

In terms of religious presuppositions (see chap. 4 for a full description), the territorialist would align well with a nature-and-grace dualism, a two-kingdoms theory, or what Niebuhr called the "Christ of culture" model. The perspectivalist position would align well with either the Christ-of-culture view or the Christ-and-culture-in-paradox view because they hold a positive view of unbiased science and culture exploration but also some recognition that the world we observe and the observer are fundamentally broken—resulting in a less-than-perfect conclusion. The integrationist view appears consistent with either the Christ-and-culture-in-paradox view or the Christ-the-transformer-of-culture view because integrationists emphasize using presuppositions to restore what may be broken within the field of psychology.

An Evaluation of the Complementary Approaches Relative to Other Approaches

All three complementary approaches take both psychology and theology seriously and on their own terms. While done in slightly different ways, each approach attempts to maintain the integrity of both science and theology. Unlike in scientific or biblical reductionism, there is no attempt to explain away one discipline using concepts from the other. Proponents of these approaches suggest that the approaches allow Christians to participate in mainstream psychological research and practice without abandoning or diminishing their Christian worldview.

23. Quoted in Ponterotto, "Qualitative Research," 129.

None of the three seeks to redefine psychological science or Christian theology, and all three require a rigorous scientific methodology in line with modern scientific psychology. This allows Christian psychologists to speak the same language as their secular counterparts, which opens avenues for collaboration and also critique. Perspectivalists like Jeeves have suggested that their view of science gives them standing to identify some of the unscientific assumptions in certain psychological theories, such as Skinner's behaviorism. By viewing scientific endeavors in the same way as non-Christians, Christians can be engaged in the larger scientific conversation and not marginalized in such discussions. As Myers puts it, "Do we really want to run off into the corner to create our own Christian psychology? By doing so do we not risk irrelevance? Are we not called to be in the world, if not of it? to be salt and light to the world? And do we not therefore need *more* Christian scholars not in the stands but down on the playing field? With an intellectual Super Bowl underway, do we not want Christians called into the game?"[24]

Proponents of all three approaches believe that participation in the larger culture is important and valuable. They argue that these approaches are preferred over both scientific and biblical reductionism because complementary approaches allow psychologists to be true to both areas of knowledge. Proponents also argue that these approaches avoid the attempt to reinvent or completely reorient psychological science or practice, as is done by humanizer approaches (see chap. 8). Often, reinventing the discipline means removing Christian psychologists from the larger conversations in the field. Finally, an advantage of taking each discipline seriously means that these approaches are more attuned to current trends and theories. As was noted in chapter 3, it is important for any model of integration to be up to date in relation to the field. One concern raised about biblical reductionism, and to a lesser extent humanizer approaches, is that it tends to criticize theories and practices that are largely outdated or passé.

Critics of the complementary approach have raised concerns that engaging in mainstream science-based psychology causes Christians to

---

24. Myers, "Levels-of-Explanation Response to Christian Psychology," 181.

compromise their worldview and to gradually capitulate to scientism and determinism. Biblical reductionists and humanizers alike have concerns that the field of psychology as it is currently practiced is based on so many worldview assumptions that are incompatible with Christian theology that either a basic transformation or a complete separation is required. Thus, critics suggest (as was quoted in chap. 4) that "the church that tries to change the world eventually becomes a church the world has changed."[25]

An Evaluation of the Complementary Approaches in Contrast to Each Other

One of the concerns about perspectivalism (as well as territorialism) is the claim that there is little or no conflict between science and theology. While in theory there should be no conflict between theology and psychology, is that true in practice? There may in fact be cases in which scientific findings challenge theological understandings of human nature. For example, contemporary concepts of gender have been seen as challenging traditional Christian views on gender. Myers has written on how, in his view, scientific research challenges a traditional Christian understanding of homosexuality.[26] These conflicts are sometimes explained away as being due to either a misunderstanding of theology or a misunderstanding of the science. Similarly, Carter and Narramore suggest that "all conflicts between theology and psychology must, therefore, be conflicts between either the facts of Scripture and the theories of psychology, the facts of psychology and our (mis)interpretation of Scripture, or between the theories of psychology and our (mis)interpretations of Scripture."[27] Whether these situations represent misunderstandings or real tensions, some type of resolution is called for.

So, if perspectivalism posits that conflicts between theology and psychology should not occur, how are apparent conflicts mediated? Which side "wins"? John Coe and Todd Hall write that a limitation of perspectivalism "is that, while it allows for complementary views

---

25. Wax, "3 Reasons."
26. See Myers and Scanzoni, *What God Has Joined Together?*
27. Carter and Narramore, *Integration of Psychology and Theology*, 22.

between the various approaches to the person, it provides no rigorous, articulated way to critique differing views or adjudicate between various vantage points. That is, if the theologian physicist and psychologist disagree about the nature of consciousness, mental experiences, dreams or teleology, there is no agreed-on methodology between them to resolve such matters."[28] While the framework of perspectivalism does not necessarily state which discipline should be deferred to, in practice, it appears that science takes precedence over theology in such conflicts. An example of this can be seen in Myers's views of homosexuality and marriage. While same-sex sexual activity (not necessarily orientation itself) has traditionally been viewed by many Christian denominations as being sinful, Myers states that "new data have, however, dragged me, along with other Christian thinkers . . . to revise my understanding of sexual orientation."[29] Myers then reviews evidence that biological factors seem to be important in sexual orientation and that efforts to change sexual orientation are quite ineffective. From this and other data he draws the conclusion that the traditional Christian understanding of homosexuality is incorrect.[30]

Another example of science taking the lead can be seen in Myers's statement about his support of family values (e.g., two-parent families, the negative effects of pornography and cohabitation). He writes, "I've always been pretty conservative on these family concerns *because the data are so persuasive*."[31] This seems to indicate that scientific findings are taking the lead in shaping his support for certain values. What if the data said otherwise? What if data arose demonstrating that cohabitation before marriage had no negative effects or even positive ones? Should this information alone cause Christians to rethink their view

28. Coe and Hall, "Transformational Psychology Response to Levels of Explanation," 92.

29. Myers, "Levels-of-Explanation View," 72.

30. We are only briefly summarizing Myers's position here due to space constraints. A full treatment of his views can be found in Myers and Scanzoni, *What God Has Joined Together?* Our point here is not to enter the debate on whether homosexual behavior is sinful, which would require a much more in-depth analysis. Rather, we are using this as an example of where science has led to a reassessment of a traditional theological view in the context of perspectivalism.

31. Myers, "Levels-of-Explanation View," 72, emphasis added.

on cohabitation, or should a Christian sexual ethic be maintained even if the data does not line up with it? The perspectivalist view does not seem to have a clear way to mediate potential conflicts like this and, in practice, appears to give undue deference to science.

Additionally, the perspectivalist view that psychological science deals with how things work (mechanisms) and that theology focuses on the greater meaning of things may be too simplistic. Theology does address meaning and value, but it also addresses practical matters, such as how one should live, and makes claims about how things work. Similarly, psychology makes several value judgments when talking about goals in therapy and the development of morality. The lines may not always be as clear as perspectivalists would like them to be. Sigmund Koch points this out by stating, "Psychology is necessarily the most philosophically-sensitive discipline in the entire gamut of disciplines that claim empirical status. We cannot discriminate a so-called variable, pose a research question, choose or invent a method, project a theory, stipulate psychotechnology, without making strong presumptions of philosophical cast about the nature of our human subject matter— presumptions that can be ordered to the age-old context of philosophical discussions."[32] This doesn't mean that theology will always have something to say about psychology or vice versa. However, there will be several instances of overlap. How do we define normal versus abnormal? What does psychological health entail? When and how should we forgive? How do we explain religious experiences? How do we understand sexuality? These are issues in psychology that seem directly related to one's values and beliefs.

The practice of clinical psychology may especially create situations where one's values and beliefs will have a direct impact on how one carries out therapy. A therapist's teleology will influence the goals and direction toward which they steer their client. One's view of mental health would seem to simultaneously involve both psychology and theology. One way that perspectivalists deal with this is to separate scientific psychology from the practice of psychology, but surely the science of psychology should inform the practice, and therefore integration in

---

32. Koch, "Nature and Limits of Psychological Knowledge," 267.

one should not be completely removed from the other. In psychology there seems to be an inevitable intermingling of values and empirical science that is not addressed if we simply view science as explaining the "how" and theology as explaining the "why."

One final concern about perspectivalism—and even more about territorialism: restricting each discipline to a certain area of under-standing human nature makes it difficult to create a unified view of human nature. It isn't clear how these separate levels or territories interact and relate to one another. Discussing the perspectivalist ap-proach, Alan Tjeltveit states, "Consistent with my Lutheran heritage, I am partly convinced that psychology and theology address differ-ent topics (or different levels of explanation), with each field of study limited in scope and restricted to the logic of its disciplinary methods. However, this approach has significant weaknesses: It fails to capture the unity of persons. I am far from convinced that current academic disciplines carve reality at its joints; they thus misunderstand us."[33]

One strength of the integrationist model can be seen in how it allows for one's Christian worldview to influence all aspects of one's work. Integrationists believe that Christian values and theology can impact research in a deeper way than is possible under a territorialist or per-spectivalist paradigm. In this sense, even though integrationists may conduct science using the same empirical tools as secular scientists, these tools are used directly alongside a Christian worldview, and the resulting psychology is distinctively Christian.

One concrete example of the differences between perspectivalists and integrationists can be seen in the different ways in which Myers and Jones interpret the data regarding sexual orientation. As described previously, Myers looks at the data and concludes that since there ap-pears to be a biological component to sexual orientation, the traditional Christian view of sexual behavior needs to be reexamined. Jones, on the other hand, looks at the data and, while agreeing that there is evidence for a biological component to sexual orientation, comes to a different conclusion. He argues that Myers overstates the evidence, but, more importantly, that even if Myers is correct in his read of the data, that

33. Tjeltveit, "Lost Opportunities, Partial Successes, and Key Questions," 19.

alone should not change the traditional Christian understanding of sexual behavior. Jones states, "The research may suggest or even prove that individuals develop certain desires or proclivities outside of their conscious choice, but the focus of Christian morality is how we act in response to God's moral law."[34] In other words, a theological understanding should be the driving force of our views on sexual behavior. Jones also points out that the traditional Christian understanding of sexuality holds that it is actual homosexual acts that are sinful, not the orientation itself. Therefore, even a biological predisposition toward homosexuality would not have to be acted on. Many factors have a biological component, such as aggressive tendencies, but we still hold people morally responsible for their aggressive behavior. So, in this case, Myers (representing the perspectivalist view) appears to view the science as deciding how we interpret theology, while Jones (representing integrationists) appears to view theology as deciding how we interpret the science.

Yet, while integrationists may give priority to theology, some argue that the predominance of theology in this approach is a weakness. Perspectivalists are concerned that allowing theology to impact things like hypothesis formation and the interpretation of data sets up a situation that biases researchers and undermines the "objectivity" of science. In fact, Jeeves raises concerns that certain forms of integration combine theology and psychology in a way that could, in his view, compromise the integrity of both. He writes, "In examining the ways in which psychologists and theologians describe basic human needs we noted how each may enrich the other but that any attempt to incorporate the one into the other is likely to lead to confusion."[35] He warns against the "unjustified intermingling of psychological concepts and religious beliefs in theory construction."[36] While Jeeves sees value in relating Christian values to the application and practice of psychology (e.g., psychotherapy), he is concerned with keeping the process of science as objective as possible. Therefore, both Myers and Jeeves would argue that imposing a theological understanding of same-sex relationships

34. Jones, "Integration View," 122.
35. Jeeves, *Human Nature at the Millennium*, 236–37.
36. Jeeves, *Human Nature at the Millennium*, 154.

will unnecessarily bias theories, hypothesis building, and data interpretation of research related to this issue. They would agree that the ultimate moral question is somewhat distinct but that the data should be as objective as humanly possible.

Relatedly, perspectivalists wonder how confident people should be in their theological interpretations. Integrationists stress the importance of Scripture and theology in guiding and shaping psychology, but this reliance is based on an assumption that they know exactly what Scripture and theology say about an issue. Myers questions this assumption by asking, "Does that fail to appreciate the extent to which biblical interpretation is a human activity that has changed over time? Yesterday's absolute biblical truths about race and gender and sexual orientation, or about what it means to be stewards of the creation, have all been revisited by more recent biblical scholarship."[37] What was an "obvious" interpretation at one time may later come into question by a different reading of Scripture.

Summary Evaluation

So, are we left with a stalemate? There are potential issues with approaches that tend to defer to science and other issues with approaches that tend to defer to theology. David Entwistle, a Christian clinical psychologist, puts forth an integrationist model that offers a more nuanced way to resolve perceived conflicts between theology and psychology. Under this framework, when a conflict appears that is not easily resolved by finding a faulty interpretation of either science or Scripture, one "should consider whether one claim is better grounded than another is (i.e., is there stronger evidence on one side of the issue?). In many instances, we can discern whether psychology or theology speaks more clearly and fully on a given issue, and when this can be done, we place more weight on that side of the issue."[38] Some teachings of Scripture are clearer and more foundational than others. For example, issues such as God as Creator, the reality of sin, and the importance

37. Myers, "Levels-of-Explanation Response to Integration," 130.
38. Entwistle, *Integrative Approaches to Psychology and Christianity*, 312.

of forgiveness are clearly attested to and accepted by most Christians. On the other hand, issues such as the nature of gender differences, principles for regulating worship, and the nature of baptism are more disputed. Similarly, some scientific theories have more support and have been more thoroughly tested than others. In Entwistle's view, if a weakly supported finding in science conflicts with a foundational Christian doctrine, then the Christian doctrine should be deferred to. If a strongly supported scientific finding conflicts with a more debated Christian stance, then the deference would shift to favor science. What about a conflict between a well-supported scientific theory and a well-accepted Christian doctrine? Entwistle suggests that we need to live with this tension when it occurs (though he thinks it will be uncommon). Other integrationists might argue that we should defer to theology in these cases because, all things being equal, they view theology as more vital to understanding human nature. In any case, Entwistle's approach represents a possible tool to begin to mediate interdisciplinary conflicts.

QUESTIONS FOR DISCUSSION

1. Which of the three complementary approaches seems most viable to you? What are your reasons for this choice? Are there certain topics that might be more amenable to one approach than another?

2. Pick a couple of the following topics and describe how the three complementary models (territorialism, perspectivalism, and integrationism) might attempt to study each one: morality, religious experiences, suffering, depression, emotions. What might the similarities and differences between the approaches be for these topics?

8

Humanizers of Science

If someone wanted to renovate their kitchen, they could take a couple different approaches. One would be to just modify or update a few things, maybe new cabinets or different countertops. The floor plan would remain the same, but the room would have an updated look. Another possibility would be to tear everything out of the kitchen and completely redesign it. The resulting new kitchen would look very different from the old one. The first method is analogous to the complementary approach to psychology discussed in the last chapter. Adherents may want to change a few things (maybe some very important things), but, overall, a Christian psychological science looks very similar to secular psychology. The humanizer[1] or rebuilder model[2] is similar to the second remodeling method. The goal of this method is to redefine what psychology is and how it is studied—in other words, to completely redesign it. As a result, Christian psychology may look very different from secular psychology. Humanizers largely agree with biblical reductionists concerning the primacy of Scripture in understanding human nature but disagree with the approach of using Scripture alone. Humanizers value empirical research from various

1. Evans, *Preserving the Person*, 89.
2. Entwistle, *Integrative Approaches to Psychology and Christianity*, 227.

disciplines, including contemporary psychology, but they believe that the strict empirical methodology of contemporary psychology is insufficient to explain human nature and behavior. While the specifics among humanizers of psychology certainly vary, the following common themes characterize this approach:

1. Values and worldview can and should affect the goals, methods, and applications of psychology.
2. Understanding human behavior requires taking human agency seriously.
3. Predicting behavior is not the same as understanding it. Understanding human behavior requires a deeper knowledge of meaning and purpose.
4. A psychology of human behavior need not and should not model itself entirely on natural science methods.

The following sections explore these four themes.

Values and Worldview

The humanizers of science perspective on integration begins by questioning whether the scientific method is truly neutral. Even in a postpositivistic view of science (see chap. 1), where there is an acknowledgment that one's presuppositions and biases can impact one's science, the goal is to try to minimize the impact of these as much as possible, thereby getting closer to a "neutral" perspective. Humanizers argue that attaining this goal is not possible or even desirable. They argue that one's presuppositions and values are necessary to fully create a Christian understanding of human nature and behavior.

They begin their argument by examining the role that values and presuppositions play in any scientific endeavor. Empirical science requires us to make assumptions that are not ultimately testable by empirical science itself. For example, you have no way of proving that what you are experiencing right now isn't an elaborate simulation. You also have no way to definitively prove that your senses are giving you an accurate representation of the world around you. You assume that you are experiencing reality and that this is not a simulation, but it is important to note that these are assumptions. Some assumptions may be more warranted than others, but they are not ultimately scientific. Certain assumptions are required to even begin the scientific process.

In terms of psychology, a naturalistic worldview underlies much of contemporary psychology, but like any worldview, naturalism contains presuppositions. The core tenet of naturalism, that everything has only a natural cause, is an untestable claim. Humanizers argue that it becomes a circular argument that ends up begging the question.[3] Saying that only evidence showing naturalistic causes will be accepted means that supernatural causes will be ignored even if they are true.[4] Therefore, the naturalistic worldview starts with as many assumptions as the theistic worldview. The very idea of trying to eliminate assumptions and value judgments from the scientific process is itself a value judgment.

The influence of presuppositions can be seen in the hypothetico-deductive method, wherein a scientist makes a hypothesis, then tests it in a way that allows for falsification. These hypotheses often come from larger theories, and the results of studies can be used to strengthen or weaken support for these theories. Yet theories themselves often contain values and presuppositions. For example, research on happiness can reveal what leads to higher levels of self-reported happiness, yet the idea that an increase in happiness is a worthy goal is a value judgment. Furthermore, one's theory will also impact how one interprets the data. For humanizers, the idea of "letting the data speak for itself" doesn't make sense. As C. Stephen Evans writes, "Theories are usually underdetermined by data, and the choice between theories that are supported equally well by empirical data must be made on the basis of value criteria which are extra-empirical."[5] This can also be seen in the argument within social psychology between those who believe that all prosocial behavior is based on self-interest and those who believe

3. See Slife and Reber, "Against Methodological Confinement."
4. Larmer, "Psychology, Theism, and Methodological Naturalism," 139.
5. Evans, *Wisdom and Humanness in Psychology*, 15.

that true altruism exists.[6] Both groups are looking at the same data but are coming to very different conclusions based on their initial theories.

Even defining concepts and measurements requires some prior understanding or presuppositions. Evans uses the example of defining anxiety.[7] If a researcher is interested in the topic of anxiety, they must define anxiety and its measurement, then decide if that measurement is truly capturing what they define as anxiety. These steps are not fully empirical and require more tools than just empirical research. These are certainly not objective, and a researcher's preexisting view of anxiety will impact how they interpret and understand what they see in others.

So, for humanizers of psychology, the question becomes not *if* values or presuppositions are impacting the scientific process but *which* values and presuppositions are impacting it. Picking the topics of study, defining concepts, and interpreting data all require more than an empirical methodology. Humanizers of science are then arguing that since a value-free science is impossible, one should simply be up front about one's values and presuppositions. Both the theist and the naturalist can openly bring their assumptions to the table because they are inevitable.[8] In some ways this is like the integrationist approach discussed in the previous chapter, but humanizers go further by stating that these values and presuppositions should impact the methods of psychology.

Human Agency

Another focus of this approach is the role of human agency. While theologians have debated the degree to which human beings have free will, there is general agreement that humans have some degree of agency and are capable of making willful choices.[9] Therefore, humanizers of science argue that a science of human behavior requires us to take agency into account. As described in chapter 1, this view often leads to

6. See Batson, "Empathy-Induced Altruistic Motivation."
7. Evans, *Wisdom and Humanness in Psychology*, 56.
8. This point is related to the question of how different worldviews can engage with one another and will be discussed in our evaluation of the humanizers' perspective.
9. Moes and Tellinghuisen, *Exploring Psychology and Christian Faith*, 19–22.

the claim that the scientific approach (i.e., positivist or postpositivist) used in the natural sciences (e.g., chemistry, physics) is insufficient for social sciences like psychology, where a more constructivist approach may be required. As Evans puts it, the humanizer of science "does not challenge the appropriateness of the hypothetico-deductive method for the natural sciences. [The humanizer] claims, however, that the particular sciences that deal with [humans], particularly those which deal with purposive human actions, are unique and should not pattern themselves on the natural sciences."[10] Christian psychologist Eric Johnson, who advocates for a more humanized approach to psychological science, points out that agents have desires, beliefs, and intentions, which differentiate them from non-agents.[11] For humanizers of science, human behavior may be regular and predictable, but it is fundamentally different from processes and concepts in the natural sciences due to agency and responsibility. Physicists and chemists can develop *laws* about their topics (e.g., under certain conditions, mixing chemical A and chemical B will have reaction X) because they are dealing with objects rather than agents. Humanizers believe that since humans are agents and have some degree of choice, science will not be able to uncover "laws of human behavior." Psychologists may be able to uncover *rules* of behavior (e.g., in situation X, most people will conform most of the time), but these rules are not determinative in the way that the laws of physics are.

Another way to think about this can be seen in Evans's discussion of events versus actions.[12] Events are regularities occurring in ways that do not require agency. Actions, however, require an agent with intentions as the cause of the actions. Evans uses an example of a falling boulder.[13] If a boulder rolls down a hill due to the erosion of the soil around it, then that is an event and is explainable by natural science and its methodology. However, if the boulder was pushed down the hill by a person, it is now an action because there was a degree of intention behind it. If that boulder hits and injures someone, we wouldn't hold

10. Evans, *Preserving the Person*, 121.
11. E. Johnson, "Human Agency and Its Social Formation," 138–39.
12. Evans, *Preserving the Person*, 70–71, 125.
13. Evans, *Preserving the Person*, 70–71.

anyone responsible for the event if it occurred due to erosion, but if a person is injured by a pushed boulder, we would hold the person who pushed it responsible because the action involved a choice by an agent. Humanizers are concerned that contemporary psychology tries to treat human actions as if they can be explained in the same way as events. With an event, if we know all the inputs, we can know what the outcome will be. Humanizers believe that knowing the inputs into a person can help predict what they might be likely to do, but due to agency, actions are not determinative in the same way non-agent events are. Johnson points out that this gets even more complicated with interpersonal interactions, since then we are dealing with the agency of more than one person.[14]

Humanizers also point out that in several clinical interventions, a degree of agency is assumed.[15] A client is approached as someone who can choose to view something from a different perspective. If the clinical realm of psychology already acknowledges some type of agency (at least implicitly), then why should researchers ignore it when trying to understand behavior?

The belief that human beings have agency can still leave room for studying behavior empirically. There may still be regularities in human behavior, and there are certainly limitations on human agency. Empirical science can be useful for both and should not be ignored. Furthermore, humanizers may argue that predictability and agency are not incompatible concepts. Being able to predict a behavior doesn't mean the behavior wasn't freely chosen. For example, a husband may be able to accurately predict what restaurant his wife will choose for dinner, but her choice is still freely made.

It should be noted that this belief in agency is a presupposition, but as discussed above, explicitly bringing one's presuppositions to the study of a phenomenon is advocated by the humanizer approach. Summarizing the arguments for and against human agency is beyond the scope of this chapter, but the topic of free will is an open question even within the naturalism-inclined field of contemporary psychology.

14. E. Johnson, "Human Agency and Its Social Formation," 140–41.
15. Howard, *Dare We Develop a Human Science?*, 52–53; and E. Johnson, *God and Soul Care*, 102.

Therefore, a researcher who is working under the assumption that human beings do not have agency is making just as much of a presupposition as the humanizer who is assuming that humans do have agency.

Meaning: Prediction versus Understanding

The issue of agency leads directly into a third point that is vital for understanding the humanizer perspective—the importance of meaning in understanding human behavior. Humanizers of science point out that merely being able to predict something is not the same as understanding it.[16] I may observe my neighbor leaving the house at 8:30 every morning and therefore come to be able to predict this behavior, but that doesn't mean I fully understand this behavior. Where is he going? Why is he going there? Is he happy or sad about having to go to this destination? I need more insight into the meaning of his behavior to fully understand it.

Similarly, even if someone was unfamiliar with the concepts of love and affection, with enough observation, they may be able to predict an action like a father giving a hug to his son. However, this would not mean that the observer would understand the meaning behind the action. Humanizers argue that to truly understand human behavior, we need to know the reasoning, motivation, and intention of the agents doing the behaviors. This makes understanding human behavior different from understanding nonhuman events in the natural sciences, such as physics or chemistry. According to Evans, there is

> a profound difference between observing events in the nonhuman natural world and observing human behavior. Of course, in the case of the nonhuman world we can observe things by applying concepts to them, and these concepts have meaning as well. But we clearly understand that the objects we observe exist independently of these meanings. Lightning was lightning long before there was any human concept of lightning. But prayer can be prayer only when people have something like a concept of prayer. Here the meaning of the event is

16. Evans, *Preserving the Person*, 133.

essential to the reality of the event in a way that is not the case for the nonhuman world.[17]

Understanding the effect of gravity on a falling rock does not require us to take the perspective of the rock, but understanding what motivates someone to seek out a relationship does require us to take the perspective of that person. We could try to look at only external factors, as behaviorists like Skinner advocated, but that would lead us to an impoverished understanding.

Psychologist George Howard puts it this way: "The judgement of observers who really know their subjects (who have not merely observed them from afar) is crucial for psychology."[18] In other words, an observer needs to have some type of shared understanding with an actor to fully grasp the meaning of an action. We may observe someone bowing their head and clasping their hands and may even be able to predict when they will do so, but without an understanding of the concept of prayer and all that goes with it, we will not understand the meaning of what they are doing. Howard argues that if human behavior is a combination of both external influences and internal agency, then the methodology of psychology needs to be more diverse than what would be used in the natural sciences.[19]

This focus on understanding behavior from the perspective of the agent certainly isn't original to humanizers of science. You may recall from chapter 3 that advocates of the humanistic school of thought in psychology have also advocated for understanding the perspective of the person. Therefore, like adherents of the humanistic approach, humanizers of science question whether current psychological research methods are capable of fully addressing the matter. They advocate for more qualitative methodology (e.g., ethnography, narrative accounts) in addition to quantitative methods. This is not to say that natural science methods are useless for psychology. These methods may discover important patterns and relationships. But they cannot provide a complete picture of the meaning or purpose from a personal perspective.

17. Evans, *Wisdom and Humanness in Psychology*, 52.
18. Howard, *Dare We Develop a Human Science?*, 54.
19. Howard, *Dare We Develop a Human Science?*, 34–39.

It is at this point that many humanizers will differ from perspectivalists and integrationists. The latter two may agree that agency is a factor but may contend that it is a part of the unexplained variation that cannot be accounted for by other factors. Humanizers reply that this just means psychological science should adapt new or additional methods.

People like Howard argue for a more phenomenological approach to research.[20] This involves a qualitative examination of the subjective experience of people and understanding the whole of a lived experience of situations rather than partitioning an experience into smaller components that can be statistically analyzed. In other words, the whole of behavior may be greater than the sum of its parts, and attempts to break it up will result in the loss of something.

An example of this more qualitative approach can be seen in the qualitative analysis of spiritual seeking done by Matthew Graham, Marvin McDonald, and Derrick Klaassen.[21] Rather than trying to measure types of religiosity by using scales and other quantitative approaches, these researchers used open-ended interviews about participants' spiritual seeking. They then composed themes based on the data and gave the theme structure to some of the participants to see if they felt it reflected their experiences. These researchers argue that this approach gave a more holistic picture of participants' experiences that would have been lost if they had tried to reduce spiritual seeking to mere numbers on a scale. As they put it, "Phenomenological investigations are needed, because phenomenology shines precisely where the sole reliance on quantitative precision becomes reductive. Rather than forcing participants to respond to pre-existing questions that point toward established categories, phenomenology is interested in the subjective lived experience of religious orientation in everyday life. We propose that qualitative research is well suited to addressing nuanced issues of the lived experience of the religious orientations in question."[22]

20. Howard, Dare We Develop a Human Science?, 172–74.

21. Graham, McDonald, and Klaassen, "Phenomenological Analysis of Spiritual Seeking."

22. Graham, McDonald, and Klaassen, "Phenomenological Analysis of Spiritual Seeking," 150.

Christian Psychology: A Transformed Science

The three principles discussed above (values, agency, and meaning) are demonstrated in a particular form of this approach called Christian Psychology. Christian Psychology is capitalized here because it refers not to a Christian view of psychology in general but rather to a specific form of integration that takes the humanizer-of-science approach. Christian Psychology views the entire concept of psychology as much broader than what is considered psychology in a modern context. Adherents view psychology as the study of human nature and behavior but do not agree with the modern conception of psychology as strictly an empirical science. They disagree that psychology started in the late 1800s with William Wundt and suggest that philosophy and theology have a rich history of examining psychology. Eric Johnson is a psychologist who has written a great deal about the Christian Psychology approach and defines Christian Psychology as "a wise science of individual human beings that includes theory building, research, teaching, training, and various kinds of practice, including the care of souls. The science flows from a Christian understanding of human nature and therefore can be distinguished from alternative versions of psychology based on different worldviews."[23]

Notice that Johnson's definition of psychology doesn't speak directly to the methodology that psychology should use. Related to the discussion of agency and meaning above, Christian Psychologists reject strictly modeling psychology after the natural sciences. For them, philosophy, theology, history, and other disciplines all offer useful tools to psychology. Rather than seeing theology and psychology as two separate things that need to be brought together through a type of integration, Christian Psychologists view the two areas as inextricably intertwined because they both deal with questions of human nature. While other views, such as perspectivalism and integrationism, maintain a clear distinction between theology and psychology, humanizers blur or eradicate the boundaries. As Johnson puts it, "The fact is that the disciplinary division between theology and psychology is not necessarily part of the order of things. It is a sociohistorically

23. E. Johnson, *Foundations for Soul Care*, 106.

constructed dichotomy that, upon reflection today, may not have been in the best interests of the Christian community. One can imagine a psychology less constrained by the methodological presumptions of modern psychology. What we need today is a single, comprehensive, holistic discipline that seeks to understand individual human beings, using all available and relevant resources."[24]

Christian Psychology, like other humanizing approaches, takes the roles of worldview and values seriously and believes that they should be foundational in the formation of psychology. Johnson notes that Christian beliefs may mean that Christian Psychologists' view of psychology differs from that of non-Christians.[25] Hopefully, there will be enough common ground for fruitful discussions, but there may be points of fundamental disagreement. For the Christian Psychologist, the goal isn't to seek acceptance from the secular scientific world. It is to understand and care for others in the way that God has called Christians to do. Certain base assumptions or control beliefs will be drawn for a Christian worldview and will act as a lens through which theories and interpretations are made. The existence of God as Creator is one of those control beliefs, and Christian Psychologists will assume this is true and construct their theories of human behavior accordingly. In this case, God's existence isn't something that needs to be proven; it is assumed. Similarly, a Christian Psychologist may assume that people have a natural tendency to sin. Interpretations of data that go against control beliefs will often be rejected in favor of interpretations that support the control beliefs.

A great deal of the work in Christian Psychology focuses on therapy. This is consistent with its general philosophy. A therapist tries to understand the context and meaning of a client's behavior and is less interested in general rules of the behavior. Humanizers argue that all behavior takes place in a specific context and has a specific meaning, and therefore it should be studied in a way that takes these things into account. Rather than being placed in artificial situations stripped of normal context and understanding, people should be studied in natural

24. E. Johnson, *Foundations for Soul Care*, 143.
25. E. Johnson, *Foundations for Soul Care*, 152.

environments, and their behavior shouldn't be reduced to observable actions and mere numbers to be statistically analyzed.[26]

Some examples of the work of Christian Psychology may help illustrate this approach. First, Robert Roberts has argued for an understanding of human emotions that considers things like agency and meaning. While many contemporary views of emotions focus primarily on the physiological and cognitive aspects of emotions, Roberts presents a model that views emotions as arising from a combination of *concerns* and *construals* in relation to a given situation.[27] So my emotional reaction to a coworker getting promoted may depend on what my primary concern is. If my primary concern is their well-being, I may experience happiness or excitement for them, but if my primary concern is my own well-being, then I may experience jealousy at being passed over myself. Additionally, if I construe the promotion as being deserved, I will likely have a different emotional response than if I construe it as being due to favoritism. Roberts's point is that to understand an emotional response, we must understand the context and the interpretation of the person experiencing it. This approach also emphasizes the possibility of agency in emotional responses. While emotions may be reactions to a given situation, changing one's concern or construal can change one's emotional responses. Roberts argues that having a Christian worldview may create a set of concerns and construals that will help people have emotional reactions that are more in line with Christian virtues such as humility, hope, and joy.

Another example of a Christian Psychology approach can be seen in James Nelson and Candice Thomason's patristic perspective of psychology, which uses the writings of early church fathers to draw forth a model of human functioning and spiritual growth.[28] They believe that "a promising possibility for a specific articulation of theism is to turn to the early Christian or *Patristic* literature, where authors developed sophisticated theistic psychologies in an attempt to understand the struggles of individuals seeking spiritual growth and inner freedom.

---

26. Van Leeuwen, *Sorcerer's Apprentice*, 116.

27. Roberts, "Emotion and the Fruit of the Spirit," 78–89.

28. Patristic literature refers to the writings of early Christians who are known as the church fathers.

These writers developed detailed understandings of psychology that provide intriguing integrations of the embodied, emotional, and spiritual aspects of life."[29] Nelson and Thomason continue, "The theistic thought of the Patristic writers allowed a view of human nature as an integrated whole, allowing writers to develop sophisticated views of development and mental illness that integrated the physical, ethical, and spiritual. Unlike some modern attempts at integration that simply add a little religious content to a current psychological theory, Patristic psychology attempts to build a complete view of the human person based on the central fact of our relationship to God."[30] While space constraints don't permit us to fully develop Nelson and Thomason's model here, they use these early writings to help describe things like depression as being related to disordered desires, weariness, or grief.

These are just a few examples of Christian Psychology. Others include using the theology of the apostle Paul to develop a therapeutic approach,[31] demonstrating how Christians and non-Christians may interpret the same measurement scale items differently,[32] and translating secular therapeutic techniques for Christian audiences.[33] These examples don't represent a full-scale rejection of secular psychology (as is the case in biblical reductionism). Rather, they are expansions of what psychology could include. The factors that hold these different examples together are a commitment to a Christian worldview and a willingness to use diverse methodologies to engage psychological questions.

In summary, Christian Psychology seeks to broaden the definition of what psychology is. Christian Psychology explicitly embraces a Christian worldview and draws its understanding of human nature and behavior from it. Christian Psychologists do not see psychology as just the scientific study of the mind and behavior using a natural science framework. They would classify any knowledge that gives insight

---

29. Nelson and Thomason, "Theistic Psychology," 96–97.
30. Nelson and Thomason, "Theistic Psychology," 99.
31. Roberts, "Outline of Pauline Psychotherapy."
32. P. Watson, "Faithful Translation and Postmodernism."
33. McFee and Monroe, "Christian Psychology Translation of Emotion-Focused Therapy."

into human behavior and relationships as being part of psychology.[34] This is not a dismissal of empirical research, which they think can be extremely helpful, but it does represent an expansion of the term *psychology* to include more than that. In this way, the resources of theology, anthropology, history, and more are seen not as something to be added to psychology but as part of psychology itself.

Worldview Foundations for Humanizers of Science

Like the complementary models in the previous chapter, humanizers' cosmology, ontology, teleology, anthropology, and axiology would likely be in line with traditional Christian thinking. However, their views on anthropology reveal some subtle differences from complementary approaches. For example, they place greater emphasis on our meaning-seeking nature, agency, and responsibility and less on the limited aspect of our choices—including the limitations that arise from our embodied nature. This is not to say that they deny our material existence, but they may give greater weight to our ability to transcend or rise above the material.

The more significant difference from the complementary models is related to epistemology, where humanizers lean toward a more constructionist approach. While they would not accept the relativism that sometimes accompanies a constructionist approach, they would embrace the notion that the mind of a person perceiving reality shapes that reality. They believe that the subjective experience one has is vital for understanding human behavior. This may be what underlies their desire for psychology to include more qualitative methodology.

An Evaluation of Humanizers of Science

For proponents of a humanizer approach, a strength is the strong Christian worldview that is allowed to permeate the theories and processes of psychology without dismissing empirical science. As a

---

34. E. Johnson, *Foundations for Soul Care*, 144–46; and Roberts, *Taking the World to Heart*, 5–7.

result, they argue, the approach avoids one of the weaknesses of biblical reductionism. Humanizers acknowledge that important information about human nature and behavior can be gained from a multitude of sources—not just Scripture. In this way, they affirm many of the same ideas that perspectivalists and integrationists support. Where they differ is that humanizers don't believe the boundaries between different disciplines are as solid as in the other approaches.

The prominent role of a Christian worldview in this approach can be seen in the belief that theology should be woven into all aspects of human experience. Theology is not something that gets added after or even before psychological work is done. Rather, it influences everything from hypothesis formation to methodology to applications. Additionally, the emphasis on clinical applications and soul care creates a more applied psychology that can have an impact on people's well-being.

Another strength is sometimes referred to as the "unity of the person."[35] Recall that one of the critiques of the perspectivalist approach is that it fragments human experience into different levels without a clear explanation of how those levels interact with one another. The humanizer approach deals with this issue by blurring the lines between the different levels and examining human experiences more phenomenologically. As previously mentioned, humanizers believe that the whole of human experience is more than the sum of its parts and that reducing things to ever smaller components causes us to lose something. So, studying emotions as a "felt experience" rather than breaking them down into physiological, cognitive, and motivational components may give us a more unified picture of what emotional experiences are.

Critics of the humanizer approach have raised concerns about broadening what is considered to be psychology. As one critic puts it, "I concur with [humanizers'] esteem for the rich insights of the ancient philosophers, of Jesus and of theologians from Augustine to Kierkegaard, but I do so without conflating them all as psychology."[36] While there are certainly different approaches to the field, there is consensus

---

35. Evans, *Preserving the Person*, 156.
36. Myers, "Levels-of-Explanation Response to Christian Psychology," 179.

that contemporary psychology is the scientific study of behavior and mental processes and that this study is done using empirical methodology. Critics argue that ethnography and narrative research in fields like history and anthropology are indeed useful, but they are not psychology. They view lumping all of these approaches and methodologies under the umbrella of psychology as a confusion of categories. By redefining psychology, humanizers run the risk of being seen as outside of or irrelevant to current psychological discourse.

Related to this is a potential concern about the applicability of Christian Psychology. Will Christian Psychology be of any interest to those outside the Christian community? Will it speak only to those who agree with the presuppositions and values that come with the Christian worldview? While proponents of a humanizer approach would argue that they are following a Christ-as-transformer-of-culture model (see chap. 4), critics have suggested that in practical terms, the approach is more like the Christ-and-culture-in-paradox approach or possibly even the Christ-against-culture approach because of the separation from mainstream circles. Some have expressed concern that this will result in a marginalization of the contributions Christians can offer the wider field. David Myers writes, "If establishment psychology is indeed where significant discoveries and new understandings are emerging, do we really want to run off into the corner to create our own Christian psychology? By doing so do we not risk irrelevance?"[37] Critics like Myers would rather see Christians have an impact on the field of psychology as it is than see them try to create a psychology of their own.

A final issue is one of expertise. Advocates of Christian Psychology have stressed that, for it to be done well, Christian Psychologists will need expertise in both the field of psychology and the field of theology.[38] This can be difficult, since very few people seek advanced studies in both. Yet, if a theorist or researcher is less of an expert in either theology or psychology, then that aspect may be less developed in their work. A theologian may lack the necessary training to fully understand psychological perspectives and research methodology, while a psychologist

37. Myers, "Levels-of-Explanation Response to Christian Psychology," 181.
38. Collins, *Psychology and Theology*.

may have a shallow theology. Territorialists and perspectivalists deal with this issue by restricting psychology and theology to separate (though related) areas. One possibility is that Christian Psychology could come about through more direct collaboration between theologians and psychologists, but in any case, the expertise issue is one that ought to be acknowledged and addressed.

Overall, humanizers' approach to psychology and theology emphasizes what they see as the unique characteristics of human beings (e.g., agency, meaning seeking). They believe that these unique factors necessitate a rebuilding or a transformation of the entire field of psychology. While they value empirical research, they do not want psychology to be bound by it, and they seek to expand the methodology of the field to include more subjective and qualitative measures. How well this approach will be accepted by those within and outside Christianity is still an open question.

QUESTIONS FOR DISCUSSION

1. Discuss the humanizers-of-science approach with a focus on the assumptions of agency and other related control beliefs. Do these factors mean we have to redefine psychology and other social sciences? Or do you believe that we should approach science the same way that natural scientists do?

2. One of the criticisms of a Christian Psychology approach is that it will isolate Christians from the broader field of psychology. Can you think of ways in which a distinct Christian psychology could be maintained while remaining engaged with the larger field?

3. Now that you have examined the different forms of integration in more depth, take some time to reflect on which one you think best suits you and why. Is it the same one you initially identified with? If you don't fit neatly into one form, how would you describe your view of integration? How will you deal with the potential tensions between psychology and faith?

Conclusion and Reflection

Reflective thinking turns experience into insight.

John C. Maxwell, *1000+ John C. Maxwell Quotes*

Reflect on what I am saying, for the Lord will give you insight into all
this.

2 Timothy 2:7

Throughout this book, we have tried to encourage reflection—on big
questions about worldviews and their impact on psychology and also
on the development of your own worldview. However, there are other
influences on worldviews that aren't based on large abstract issues.
Applying faith to practice is more than having a set of abstract theories
or propositions; it is also a lived experience. The way our worldviews
develop and the way we apply them to psychology are also influenced
by our emotions, the nature of our relationships with colleagues or
clients, our own experiences of struggle, and our own spiritual journey.
In other words, there are very intangible but nonetheless real personal
elements to integrating faith with psychology. In addition, regardless of
the specific model of integration, most Christians working in the field
of psychology would agree that part of applying a Christian worldview involves behaving ethically in one's work and treating people
as we would want to be treated. So in this conclusion we explore the

influence of personal experiences, the nature of relationships with others in professional work, and what it means to enter a "Christian vocation."

Personal Background

As we described in chapter 2, our personhood is defined relationally, so part of applying faith to psychology involves understanding how we relate to others in and through our work. Our own cultural background is one influence that can profoundly shape how we understand and relate to others. David Smith, in his book *Learning from the Stranger*, recounts the story told by Jesus of the good Samaritan, who was the only person willing to help a robbed and beaten Jewish traveler. Smith reminds us that not only were the Samaritans culturally different from the Israelites but they were religious, political, and social rivals—who were often hated by the Jews. Yet Jesus holds up the Samaritan as the person who "loved his neighbor as himself." Smith uses this story to remind us that we need to understand our own culture—with its treasures as well as its baggage—to understand how to relate to others and how we too can love our neighbor as ourselves.

Christian counseling psychologist Joshua Hook puts this into practice by promoting cultural humility rather than cultural competence. Competence suggests some end point that involves mastery over a skill, which he says can lead to a sense that one's worldview is superior. Cultural humility is much different: "On the intrapersonal level, cultural humility involves an awareness of the limitations in our ability to understand the worldview and cultural background of our client. On the interpersonal level, cultural humility involves a stance toward the client that is other oriented, marked by respect and openness to the client's worldview."[1]

He goes on to stress that applying one's faith to psychology is more than a method; it is also a stance of respect for those who might be different from us. Hook suggests that this cultural humility allows him to truly connect with clients, which he feels is important for growth.

---

1. Hook, "Engaging Clients with Cultural Humility," 278.

This principle would also apply to any human service profession. So, showing hospitality to the stranger requires understanding one's culturally based worldviews and how these perspectives might be very different from the perspectives of the other.

In addition to cultural values, our emotional, social, and spiritual struggles influence how we apply our faith to our work and how we relate to clients or colleagues. Personal struggles can be harmful or helpful. Author and ordained pastor Kathryn Greene-McCreight experienced a deep and very dark depression.[2] This led to many spiritual struggles, as she questioned why God would allow her to experience such suffering. It also created difficulties in her personal and professional lives. However, she also gained a much deeper appreciation for those in her congregation who had similar struggles and was better able to provide support and guidance to others.

Personal struggles can help us appreciate the difficulties others face. Individuals who have experienced the loss of a spouse, who have a child struggling with sexual identity, who have struggled with addiction, or who have received a diagnosis of cancer often have a very different point of view on these issues compared to others who have not experienced them. This does not mean that one perspective is inherently better than another, but there is little question that our experiences impact how we understand and relate to others.

All this comes down to empathy. Regardless of the area of psychology or service you might pursue, the method of therapy you might practice, or the types of clients you might serve, empathy is a foundational Christian practice. As theologian Kathleen Cahalan suggests, "Culturally, the dominant appeal to serve the neighbor is by way of compassion and empathy, the deep fellow-feeling that we can understand and feel with the suffering of others. Once we feel with another, we are moved to do something about it."[3] This does not mean that professionals must become emotionally immersed in their clients' concerns (since a measure of professional detachment is needed in many cases). But it does imply that we are not properly

2. Greene-McCreight, *Darkness Is My Only Companion*, 102–11.
3. Cahalan, "Callings over a Lifetime," 27–28.

motivated to provide the help needed unless we truly appreciate the suffering of others.

Professional Ethics

Applying faith to psychology also implies a personal commitment to ethical behavior. Being honest and trustworthy in our dealings is a basic tenet of Scripture.[4] Treating others as we would want to be treated is one of the central messages of the gospel.[5] Special consideration is also needed for those who are disadvantaged by poverty, social class, disability, race, or gender.[6] Thankfully, almost all programs that prepare individuals for professional counseling or clinical work give training in ethical practice, and most professional organizations that provide licensing have strict guidelines concerning confidentiality, sexual harassment, and appropriate boundaries. Likewise, researchers conducting research at universities or clinics must adhere to strict guidelines regarding confidentiality and safeguarding the rights of participants. Christian researchers need to remind themselves that they must collect data honestly and must not misrepresent the data. Therapists need to be honest with clients and supervisors. These are basic moral principles, but they are very integral when applying faith to one's work.

Entering a "Christian Vocation"

Early in the book, we spoke of teleology and axiology as ways of thinking about theories and practices in psychology, but these concepts can be applied personally as well. If you are a student about to complete formal education, you must be mindful about the purpose of your work as you begin to apply your values and your faith to your vocation. What do we mean by vocation? First, we are not thinking of vocation as a

---

4. Deuteronomy 25:15: "You must have accurate and honest weights and measures, so that you may live long in the land the LORD your God is giving you."
5. Matthew 7:12: "So in everything, do to others what you would have them do to you, for this sums up the Law and the Prophets."
6. Matthew 25:40: "Truly I tell you, whatever you did for one of the least of these brothers and sisters of mine, you did for me."

job or even a particular professional area. Rather, as Cahalan suggests, vocation implies *calling*.[7] The church reformer Martin Luther distinguishes between a general calling, which is God's call to all believers to live holy lives of service, and a particular calling, which is related to the gifts and talents of the individual. Cahalan says that both types of calling are relational in nature but that our general calling is the most relational. She states that "we experience God's callings through others and for others as the way we embody self-giving love in community. Vocation, then, is a way in which God calls persons to be in relationship to and for one another."[8] However, she laments the cultural shifts that have taken place concerning calling: "But modernity shifted the relationship between the general calling and the particular calling. We live in the age of the particular calling rather than the general calling. Modernity's turn to the subject has meant that a sense of general calling shared with others is secondary to my own pursuit."[9]

Cahalan is quick to point out that young adults trying to understand their particular calling need not assume that they need to identify the *one* work or activity to which God has called them. Callings can change over time and over circumstances. We are free to engage in a dynamic exploration of our purposes and know that there are many ways we can be of service—in particular and in general.

Community is how we apply our calling, but it is also how we remain focused on the primary purpose of our work and the values we hold dear. To maintain this focus, Christian psychologist Elizabeth Lewis Hall suggests that we need to be grounded in a redeemed community. For Hall, this means being immersed in a church body but also being participants in a community of like-minded professionals who can be "salt and light" to the broader psychological community.[10] Hall also believes that we need to develop theological grounding so that we do not lose sight of the larger purpose of our work and the ways that our values can be put to good use. Finally, she encourages young adults

7. Cahalan, "Callings over a Lifetime," 12.
8. Cahalan, "Callings over a Lifetime," 25.
9. Cahalan, "Callings over a Lifetime," 25.
10. M. Elizabeth Lewis Hall, "God as Cause or Error? Academic Psychology as Christian Vocation," *Journal of Psychology and Theology* 32, no. 3 (2004): 205.

just entering their professions to practice humility but also to question the status quo and to rethink the standard paradigms within the field of psychology.[11]

In the end, vocation is about pursuing the larger communal good. Vocation is more than being of service to others; it's being in solidarity with them. As Cahalan notes, "A relational and communal view of vocation means that we are called to be agents of vocation in turn—identifying others' gifts, affirming and nurturing them, and supporting institutional structures that allow everyone's callings to flourish."[12]

Whether or not you pursue some form of social service or clinical application, you could consider using your knowledge, gifts, and perspectives to be agents of change in your church, your community, or your institution. For example, we know individuals who have trained as Stephen's Ministers. This layperson's ministry is designed to help parishioners become equipped to walk beside people who are grieving, who are struggling with their purpose in life, or who just need someone to talk to. This program trains individuals not to be therapists or to provide advice but to simply be available and caring. This is just one of the thousands of ways you can pursue the larger communal good as part of your general and particular calling.

Regardless of your particular worldview or your particular model of integration, we pray that you will find your purpose and apply your gifts, talents, and knowledge to the greater communal good and for the furtherance of God's kingdom.

11. Hall, "God as Cause or Error?," 200–209.
12. Cahalan, "Callings over a Lifetime," 29.

Appendix

What Is a Person?

In chapter 2 we briefly discussed issues concerning anthropology and ontology (i.e., What are humans, and of what substance are we made?). We described three basic positions about human nature: (1) monism combined with materialism (i.e., humans are of one substance, and we are nothing but that physical substance), (2) monism combined with the notion of an "emergent property" (i.e., we are one substance, but we are more than the sum of our physical parts), and (3) dualism (i.e., humans are composed of two distinct substances or "realities"). As we described earlier, the third position has been the dominant view among most people in the world and particularly of most Christians. Therefore, many students may struggle with understanding the second position and how it might even be plausible within the Christian context. In this appendix, we focus on the latter two positions because—for most persons of faith—these are the only reasonable positions to take within a religious context. We expand on these issues here because of their complexity.

We must confess that our own leaning is toward position number 2, monism (although the strength of that leaning is not equal between the two of us). But our goal in this appendix is not to persuade readers of the second position; we are fully aware that many brilliant, dedicated, and orthodox theologians, Christian scientists, and biblical scholars come to different conclusions on this issue. Instead, our goal is to explain why some Christian scholars feel that this position is scientifically more tenable, philosophically workable, and—most importantly—consistent with proper biblical interpretation. Using both biblical reasons and philosophical ones, we will also present arguments against this position and explain why many scholars hold to a more "traditional" understanding of human nature.

Why do we bother to take on this tricky and perhaps—as some would say—unanswerable question? Because, as we alluded to in chapter 2, one's view has significant implications for how one views the science of human behavior, how one views psychological disorder, how one might approach therapy, and even how one approaches the wider culture. Even though some of the information we present in this appendix is not directly pertinent to these questions, a deeper dive into the philosophical, scientific, or theological reasons given for these positions is necessary so that students have a full understanding of why people take these positions—and how they might approach them in the future.

Mind and Brain

Before talking about the soul, we focus on the mind and whether using that word is simply a way of talking about the activity of the brain or whether the mind operates outside the natural world. If you have been a student of psychology for some time, you are perhaps aware of the tight link between brain activity and our conscious experience. In fact, you don't really need to be a psychologist or a neuroscientist to see this relationship because you experience it daily. Every time you go to sleep and every time you wake up, you detect the tight link between brain activity and conscious awareness. Indeed, sleep researchers Jose Cantero and Mercedes Atienza have confirmed that the synchronization of nerve cells (i.e., firing impulses with similar patterns at the same time) creates different states of consciousness during sleep and wakefulness: "Growing evidence prompts the thought that different levels of cerebral integration mediated by various scales of spatial and temporal synchrony over multiple frequency bands could play a key functional role in the emergence of percepts, memories, emotions, thoughts, and actions."[1]

There is little debate that our mental activity, including our conscious awareness, is entirely dependent on brain activity. Christian neuroscientist Malcolm Jeeves also describes countless cases of brain injury or brain changes that can profoundly impact personality, moral character, and even religious belief.[2] In addition, he describes famous cases of "split brain" surgery in which the major nerve fibers that connect the left and right cerebral hemispheres are cut to control epileptic seizures. In these cases, individuals appear to have two separate conscious experiences in the left and right hemispheres. So if you place a plastic mold of the number three in the left hand of a blindfolded person with a split brain, they can signal the number three using the fingers of their left hand, but when asked to give a verbal answer, they can only guess. This is because the left hand sends information to only the nonspeaking right hemisphere—so the disconnected left (speaking) hemisphere has no conscious awareness of the number. Jeeves and others ask, If the mind were somehow not part of the material world, then why would creating a physical disconnection cause a disconnection of consciousness in the nonmaterial world (i.e., couldn't the thought still "pass" from one part of the mind to the other if the thought exists outside material substance)?

But if we accept that the mind is part of the material world, does this require us to accept the naturalist, materialist, and deterministic views of some psychologists? In other words, are we nothing but what our neurons do, and therefore we have no agency or responsibility? For many secular scientists, as we described earlier, the answer is clearly yes. However, a significant number of Christian and a small number of non-Christian psychologists have suggested that the answer is no. These individuals promote the concepts of emergent property (i.e., that the mind emerges from the complex interaction of brain mechanisms) and supervenience (i.e., mental properties arising from brain

1. Cantero and Atienza, "Role of Neural Synchronization," 69.
2. Jeeves, *Human Nature at the Millennium*, 42–59.

activity are capable of exerting "downward causation" on lower-level mechanisms). These same individuals propose a concept called non-reductive physicalism, which suggests that we are physical entities but that we cannot be reduced to physical components. In this way they avoid reductionism but also leave room for agency (i.e., free will) and responsibility. Even secular psychologists Martin Seligman and colleagues have offered a possible mechanism for possessing agency or free will that they refer to as "prospection" or the ability to contemplate future events independent of past causes. They state:

> There is one sense of "will" that comes into play when we engage in the spontaneous or deliberate prospection of future possibilities. This feels "free" because the mind freely explores possibilities, and it feels like "freely willing" because what precipitates our action is the making up of our mind among these alternatives. Nothing more, no additional act of will, is required to act "as I see fit." So the experience of "freely willing" is running through these prospections until one feels that one's mind is made up and then taking the course of action one has settled on, and nothing more. The "settled outcome" is in an obvious sense one's own idea, because it came about through one's own unimpeded mental activity, without internal compulsion (which is insensitive to what one prefers) or external coercion (which prevents one from weighing options without interference) or overpowering temptation (in which case the agent does not have the will he wants). No transcendental will is needed for the act to be "of one's own accord"; no rational homunculus must "freely endorse" it—for when the agent settles his mind after freely exploring options by following what "seems best," then if the agent also wants to have this be the ground of his choice, that is the agent freely endorsing it in every relevant sense and performing the act because of his endorsement.[3]

These authors admit that they have not settled any metaphysical question about whether the mind is material or immaterial, but they believe that prospection meets all the criteria for how one might account for human agency without reference to a rational homunculus (i.e., nonmaterial mind).

3. Seligman et al., "Navigating into the Future," 133.

Body, Mind, and Soul

Even many Christian philosophers and biblical scholars who hold to a dualist position regarding the human person acknowledge that much of what we know about neuroscience shows a strong relationship between brain and mind. For example, Christian philosopher Stephen Evans, who favors a form of minimal dualism, suggests that in this life, brain and mind occupy the same space and time and that the mind is entirely dependent on brain function for existence while we are alive.[4] Likewise, biblical scholar John Cooper argues that in this life, mind and brain are one but that at death, God "extracts" our mind (i.e., soul). Therefore, during the "intermediate state" between death and resurrection, people can exist as disembodied souls.[5] Christian monists, however, argue that there is no reason to account for any form of separation in this life or the next. They contend that Scripture paints a very different picture than has been traditionally portrayed and that many of our past and current Bible translations and interpretations have been heavily influenced by Greek philosophy (e.g., the dual view of body and soul as proposed by Plato). Time does not allow us to give a full description of these issues, but we can summarize some of the basic theological and biblical arguments against Cartesian (i.e., proposed by René Descartes) dualism.

The Basic Arguments concerning Biblical Translation

First, throughout Scripture, the words in the Old and New Testaments (*nephesh* and *psychē*, respectively) that are sometimes translated into English as "soul" can also be translated as "living being," "mind," or "person" (even within the same version or translation of Scripture, such as the NIV). For example, the Hebrew word *nephesh* in the Old Testament—which is sometimes translated as "soul"—is also applied to mammals (e.g., Gen. 1:30; Lev. 11:46; Job 12:10), fish, and birds (e.g., Gen. 1:20; Lev. 11:10). In the New Testament, the word *psychē*

4. Evans, "Separable Souls."
5. See Cooper, "Biblical Anthropology Is Holistic and Dualistic"; and Cooper, *Body, Soul, and Life Everlasting.*

is sometimes translated as "soul" but other times as "mind" or simply "person." Even Cooper, who argues for a form of dualism at death, has suggested that "the overall picture of the Hebrew anthropology, therefore, is that humans are holistically constituted as integrated psychophysical unities. There is little room in the Old Testament for construing soul and body in the Platonic metaphysical categories of spiritual and material substance."[6] So, the words translated as "soul" may not mean what we typically think they mean, and many believe they simply refer to a living, breathing (i.e., material) being.

Second, many passages, especially in the New Testament, that appear to suggest the separation of body and soul may be mistranslated or misinterpreted from the original intent of the author.[7]

Third, the early church fathers and translators of Scripture were heavily influenced by the prevailing Greek philosophy of the day. As a result, says biblical scholar Joel Green, early translations placed a different connotation on the words and phrases that were used to convey concepts such as mind, person, and living being.[8]

In addition to these arguments concerning biblical interpretation and translation, many Christian neuroscientists have argued that the Cartesian view is both unnecessary to maintain some form of free will and increasingly impossible to square with contemporary neuroscience. What about essential doctrines of the faith, such as the resurrection and life after death? Christian monists often point out that a central tenet of the Christian faith is the resurrection of the body. Therefore, they argue, the body is essential to understanding personhood and needs to be emphasized more in our theology. What about the time between death and resurrection? This issue gets particularly difficult to comprehend, but many have proposed various solutions to this quandary. Some have suggested that there is no separation between body and mind-soul in this life but that God extracts some form of nonmaterial essence at death.[9] Others have proposed something called

6. Cooper, "Body-Soul Question," 5.
7. J. Green, "Bodies."
8. For examples, see J. Green, "Bodies"; and Wright, "Mind, Spirit, Soul and Body."
9. For examples, see Cooper, *Body, Soul, and Life Everlasting*; and Evans, "Separable Souls."

immediate resurrection, which suggests that when we die, we step not only out of this life but out of time and space as we know them. Therefore, we are resurrected and re-created with new bodies instantly at the time of death. In this scheme, we cannot exist—in this life or in the next—without a bodily existence.[10]

To summarize, these Christian monists believe that God created us from the dust as mortals and that we are not made of "parts" (i.e., body-mind or body-soul) put together but are whole, unified beings who are still capable of willful action. As biblical scholar and theologian N. T. Wright states:

> My basic proposal, as is already apparent, is that we need to think in terms of a *differentiated unity*. Paul and the other early Christian writers didn't reify their anthropological terms. Though Paul uses his language with remarkable consistency, he nowhere suggests that any of the key terms refers to a particular "part" of the human being to be played off against any other. Each *denotes* the entire human being, while *connoting* some angle of vision on who that human is and what he or she is called to be. Thus, for instance, *sarx*, flesh, refers to the entire human being but connotes corruptibility, failure, rebellion, and then sin and death. *Psychē* denotes the entire human being, and connotes that human as possessed of ordinary mortal life, with breath and blood sustained by food and drink. And so on. No doubt none of the terms is arbitrary; all would repay further study.[11]

Wright's notion of a differentiated unity stresses that we have a variety of qualities of being but that Scripture is not speaking of parts or entities that are somehow combined to form a human being.

Of course, a wide variety of Christian philosophers and theologians with astute minds have argued forcefully for either a partial[12] or a complete form of body/soul dualism, and they believe that this position is still compatible with neuroscience findings and is more compatible with scriptural interpretation. Christian philosophers such as David Aiken, James B. Stump, and Adam Wood, who represent a variety of

---

10. See J. Green, "Bodies."
11. Wright, "Mind, Spirit, Soul and Body," 471.
12. Evans refers to his view as "minimal dualism." Evans, "Separable Souls," 27.

Christian institutions and theological backgrounds, have argued that to
understand human agency and the concept of being made in the image
of God, we must maintain some form of dualistic understanding of the
person.[13] They argue that it is incompatible with a Christian understanding of both God and humans to propose that a mind, or human
intelligence, cannot exist without a body because doing so would deny
that God—who is spirit (and not embodied)—can have a mind.

Conclusions and Applications

This brief expansion of ideas related to brains, minds, souls, and persons is still very insufficient to capture all the arguments and rationales
for these various positions. Therefore, we encourage you to explore
several of the readings referenced in this appendix for further understanding. But given that there is continued disagreement among very
learned and committed Christian scholars, you may wonder how the
average educated layperson is supposed to make sense of all this. You
may also wonder if it is worth the effort to explore these issues further when it seems about as fruitful and useful as arguing about the
number of angels who can dance on the head of a pin. We understand
this sentiment completely, but we do believe there are some important
issues that need to be understood regardless of any specific conclusion
about the nature of the soul.

For example, despite significant disagreement about the particulars
of philosophy and theology, virtually all the authors mentioned in this
appendix emphasize the need to rediscover the scriptural emphasis on
our bodily existence. For example, Cooper, who still argues for some
form of dualism in Christian anthropology, also contends that the more
damaging Greek form of dualism has caused Christians over the centuries to devalue emotions (which are bodily and evil) and to see many
of our basic motivations (i.e., sexual desires) as inherently evil, while
rational thought—which resides in the soul—is relatively unaffected
by sin. He states, "As a result, body, mind, emotions, and spirit have

13. See Aiken, "Why I Am Not a Physicalist"; Stump, "Non-Reductive Physicalism";
and Wood, "Disembodied Souls without Dualism."

been cut off from each other both in ordinary life and in our attempts to treat the problems of ordinary life. People compartmentalize their minds from their emotions and their emotions from physical and spiritual expression. This dualism is a factor even in the ecological crisis, for we have treated the earth as mere matter. This mind-body dualism must be eradicated. We must return to a more holistic, integrated way of understanding ourselves."[14]

This is only one of the many ideas expressed about these issues. Individuals often have much more nuanced and complex positions than have been described here, so you should view these ideas as being on a continuum, with dualism on one end and monism on the other. However, Cooper raises issues here that underscore why this is important for students to grapple with. Agree or disagree with his point of view, you can see that models of integration that stress spirituality are clearly more on the side of some form of dualism, while models of integration that stress scientific approaches in addition to theological or scriptural understanding often lean toward a more monistic or holistic view of the person. If the mind-soul is distinct from the body, and if we can transcend or overrule our bodily motives and emotions, then care of the *psychē* will need to focus on soul care. If the mind (or soul) is just a quality of the whole person, then care of the *psychē* can focus on spiritual understanding and also on the scientific understanding of how mental activity occurs.

QUESTIONS FOR DISCUSSION

1. If one were to adopt a more holistic view of our embodied nature, is it still useful to talk about the spiritual life? Why or why not?
2. If one were to eliminate the traditional view of soul from our language, what would make humans special in relation to the rest of the living world—or is there nothing special about humans?

14. Cooper, "Body-Soul Question," 3.

Bibliography

Adams, Jay E. "The Big Umbrella." In *Essays on Counseling*, edited by Jay E. Adams, 2–35. Grand Rapids: Zondervan, 1986.

———. *The Christian Counselor's Manual: The Practice of Nouthetic Counseling*. New York: HarperCollins, 1986.

———. *Competent to Counsel: Introduction to Nouthetic Counseling*. Grand Rapids: Zondervan, 1986.

Aiken, David W. "Why I Am Not a Physicalist: A Dialogue, a Meditation, and a Cumulative Critique." *Christian Scholar's Review* 33, no. 2 (2004): 165.

Archer, Margaret, Roy Bhaskar, Andrew Collier, Tony Lawson, and Alan Norrie. *Critical Realism: Essential Readings*. New York: Routledge, 2013.

Bargh, John A., and Melissa J. Ferguson. "Beyond Behaviorism: On the Automaticity of Higher Mental Processes." *Psychological Bulletin* 126, no. 6 (2000): 925–45.

Barret, Justin. "Cognitive Science, Religion, and Theology." In *The Believing Primate: Scientific, Philosophical, and Theological Reflections on the Origin of Religion*, edited by Jeffrey Schloss and Michael Murray, 76–99. Oxford: Oxford University Press, 2009.

Barth, Karl. *Church Dogmatics*. Vol. III/1. London: A&C Black, 2004.

Baschera, Luca. "Total Depravity? The Consequences of Original Sin in John Calvin and Later Reformed Theology." In *Calvinus Clarissimus Theologus*, edited by Herman J. Selderhuis, 37–58. Göttingen: Vandenhoeck & Ruprecht, 2012.

Batson, C. Daniel. "Empathy-Induced Altruistic Motivation." In *Prosocial Motives, Emotions, and Behavior: The Better Angels of Our Nature*, edited by Mario Mikulincer and Phillip R. Shaver, 15–34. Washington, DC: American Psychological Association, 2010.

Baumeister, Roy F., and Kathleen D. Vohs. "Revisiting Our Reappraisal of the (Surprisingly Few) Benefits of High Self-Esteem." *Perspectives on Psychological Science* 13, no. 2 (2018): 137–40.

Bendroth, Margaret. "Christian Fundamentalism in America." *Oxford Research Encyclopedia of Religion*. February 27, 2016. https://doi.org/10.1093/acrefore /9780199340378.013.419.

Benz, Ernst. *The Eastern Orthodox Church: Its Thought and Life*. New York: Routledge, 2017. First published 1957 by Transaction Publishers.

Berg, Christian. "Leaving Behind the God-of-the-Gaps: Towards a Theological Response to Scientific Limit Questions." In *Expanding Humanity's Vision of God: New Thoughts on Science and Religion*, edited by Robert L. Herrmann, 87–116. Philadelphia: Templeton Foundation Press, 2001.

Boettner, Loraine. *The Reformed Doctrine of Predestination*. 1901. Reprint, San Francisco: Pickle Partners Publishing, 2017.

Bratt, James D., ed. *Abraham Kuyper: A Centennial Reader*. Grand Rapids: Eerdmans, 1998.

Brown, Warren S. "Cognitive Contributions to Soul." In Brown, Murphy, and Malony, *Whatever Happened to the Soul?*, 99–125.

Brown, Warren S., Nancey Murphy, and H. Newton Malony, eds. *Whatever Happened to the Soul? Scientific and Theological Portraits of Human Nature*. Minneapolis: Fortress, 1998.

Brown, Warren S., and Brad D. Strawn. *The Physical Nature of Christian Life: Neuroscience, Psychology, and the Church*. Cambridge: Cambridge University Press, 2012.

Bulbulia, Joseph. "The Cognitive and Evolutionary Psychology of Religion." *Biology and Philosophy* 19, no. 5 (2004): 655–86.

Burke, Brian L., Andy Martens, and Erik H. Faucher. "Two Decades of Terror Management Theory: A Meta-Analysis of Mortality Salience Research." *Personality and Social Psychology Review* 14, no. 2 (2010): 155–95.

Cahalan, Kathleen A. "Callings over a Lifetime." In *Calling All Years Good: Christian Vocation throughout Life's Seasons*, by Kathleen A. Cahalan and Bonnie J. Miller-McLemore, 12–32. Grand Rapids: Eerdmans, 2017.

Cantero, Jose L., and Mercedes Atienza. "The Role of Neural Synchronization in the Emergence of Cognition across the Wake-Sleep Cycle." *Reviews in the Neurosciences* 16, no. 1 (2005): 69–84.

Carson, Donald A. *Christ and Culture Revisited.* Grand Rapids: Eerdmans, 2012.

Carter, John D., and Bruce Narramore. *The Integration of Psychology and Theology: An Introduction.* Grand Rapids: Zondervan, 1979.

Chóliz, Mariano. "Experimental Analysis of the Game in Pathological Gamblers: Effect of the Immediacy of the Reward in Slot Machines." *Journal of Gambling Studies* 26, no. 2 (2010): 249–56.

Chomsky, Noam. *What Kind of Creatures Are We?* New York: Columbia University Press, 2015.

Cochran, Robert, Jr. *Faith and Law: How Religious Traditions from Calvinism to Islam View American Law.* New York: New York University Press, 2008.

Coe, John H., and Todd W. Hall. "A Transformational Psychology Response to Levels of Explanation." In Johnson, *Psychology and Christianity*, 90–95.

Collins, Gary R. *Psychology and Theology: Prospects for Integration.* Nashville: Abingdon, 1981.

Cooper, John W. "Biblical Anthropology Is Holistic and Dualistic." In *The Blackwell Companion to Substance Dualism*, edited by Jonathan Loose, Angus Menuge, and J. P. Moreland, 411–26. Hoboken, NJ: Wiley, 2018.

———. *Body, Soul, and Life Everlasting: Biblical Anthropology and the Monism-Dualism Debate.* Grand Rapids: Eerdmans, 2000.

———. "Body-Soul Question: Can We Be Both Confessional and Reformational?" *Pro Rege* 20, no. 1 (1991): 1–12.

Cullen, Dallas. "Feminism, Management, and Self-Actualization." *Gender, Work & Organization* 1, no. 3 (1994): 127–37.

Curran, Charles E. *Catholic Social Teaching, 1891–Present: A Historical, Theological, and Ethical Analysis.* Washington, DC: Georgetown University Press, 2002.

Davis, Nicola. *An Analysis of Richard Dawkins's "The Selfish Gene."* London: Taylor & Francis, 2017.

Del Colle, Ralph. "Miracles in Christianity." In *Cambridge Companion to Miracles*, edited by Graham H. Twelftree, 235–53. Cambridge: Cambridge University Press, 2011.

Ebersole, Peter, and Greg DeVore. "Self-Actualization, Diversity, and Meaning in Life." *Journal of Social Behavior and Personality* 10, no. 1 (1995): 37.

Entwistle, David N. *Integrative Approaches to Psychology and Christianity: An Introduction to Worldview Issues, Philosophical Foundations, and Models of Integration.* 4th ed. Eugene, OR: Wipf & Stock, 2021.

Evans, C. Stephen. *Preserving the Person: A Look at the Human Sciences.* Vancouver, BC: Regent College Publishing, 1994.

———. "Separable Souls: Dualism, Selfhood, and the Possibility of Life after Death." *Christian Scholar's Review* 34, no. 3 (2005): 327–40.

———. *Wisdom and Humanness in Psychology: Prospects for a Christian Approach.* Grand Rapids: Baker, 1989.

Fenichel, Otto. *The Psychoanalytic Theory of Neurosis.* New York: Routledge, 2014.

Finger, Thomas N. *A Contemporary Anabaptist Theology: Biblical, Historical, Constructive.* Downers Grove, IL: InterVarsity, 2010.

Frair, Wayne F., and Gary D. Patterson. *Science and Christianity: Four Views.* Downers Grove, IL: InterVarsity, 2000.

Fraser, J. Cameron. *Developments in Biblical Counseling.* Grand Rapids: Reformation Heritage Books, 2015.

Funk, Ken. "What Is a Worldview?" March 21, 2001. http://web.engr.oregon state.edu/~funkk/Personal/worldview.html.

Gould, Stephen Jay. "Nonoverlapping Magisteria." *Natural History* 106, no. 2 (1997): 16–22.

Graham, Matthew D., Marvin J. McDonald, and Derrick W. Klaassen. "A Phenomenological Analysis of Spiritual Seeking: Listening to Quester Voices." *International Journal for the Psychology of Religion* 18, no. 2 (2008): 146–63.

Green, Christopher D. "Darwinian Theory, Functionalism, and the First American Psychological Revolution." *American Psychologist* 64, no. 2 (2009): 75–83.

Green, Joel B. "'Bodies—That Is, Human Lives': A Re-Examination of Human Nature in the Bible." In Brown, Murphy, and Malony, *Whatever Happened to the Soul?*, 149–72.

Greene-McCreight, Kathryn. *Darkness Is My Only Companion: A Christian Response to Mental Illness.* Grand Rapids: Brazos, 2015.

Groves, Alasdair, and Todd Stryd. "Methodology." April 16, 2019. Podcast from the Christian Counseling and Educational Foundation. MP3 audio. 21:28. https://www.ccef.org/podcast/methodology/.

Gunnoe, Marjorie Lindner. *The Person in Psychology and Christianity: A Faith-Based Critique of Five Theories of Social Development.* Downers Grove, IL: InterVarsity, 2022.

Guthrie, Stewart Elliott. *Faces in the Clouds: A New Theory of Religion.* Oxford: Oxford University Press, 1995.

Haggbloom, Steven J., Renee Warnick, Jason E. Warnick, Vinessa K. Jones, Gary L. Yarbrough, Tenea M. Russell, Chris M. Borecky et al. "The 100 Most Eminent Psychologists of the 20th Century." *Review of General Psychology* 6, no. 2 (2002): 139–52.

Hall, Elizabeth Lewis. "God as Cause or Error? Academic Psychology as Christian Vocation." *Journal of Psychology and Theology* 32, no. 3 (2004): 200–209.

———. "What Are Bodies For? An Integrative Examination of Embodiment." *Christian Scholar's Review* 39, no. 2 (2010): 159–75.

Hamilton, D. "Traditions, Preferences, and Postures." In *The SAGE Handbook of Qualitative Research,* 1st ed., edited by Norman K. Denzin and Yvonna S. Lincoln, 60–69. Thousand Oaks, CA: Sage, 1994.

Henderson, John. "A Definition for Biblical Counseling." Association of Biblical Counselors, August 2, 2021. https://christiancounseling.com/blog/definition-biblical-counseling/.

Hilgard, Ernest R. *Psychology in America: A Historical Survey.* San Diego: Harcourt Brace Jovanovich, 1987.

Hook, Joshua N. "Engaging Clients with Cultural Humility." *Journal of Psychology and Christianity* 33, no. 3 (2014): 277–81.

Howard, George S. *Dare We Develop a Human Science?* Notre Dame, IN: Academic Publications, 1986.

James, William. *Pragmatism and Four Essays from the Meaning of Truth.* New York: World Publishing, 1909.

———. *Psychology.* New York: Henry Holt, 1892.

———. *The Will to Believe: And Other Essays in Popular Philosophy, and Human Immortality.* New York: Dover, 1956.

Jeeves, Malcolm A. *Human Nature at the Millennium: Reflections on the Integration of Psychology and Christianity.* Downers Grove, IL: InterVarsity, 1997.

Jeeves, Malcolm A., and Thomas E. Ludwig. *Psychological Science and Christian Faith: Insights and Enrichments from Constructive Dialogue.* West Conshohocken, PA: Templeton Foundation Press, 2018.

Johnson, Eric L. *Foundations for Soul Care: A Christian Psychology Proposal.* Downers Grove, IL: InterVarsity, 2007.

———. *God and Soul Care: The Therapeutic Resources of the Christian Faith.* Downers Grove, IL: InterVarsity, 2017.

——. "Human Agency and Its Social Formation." In *Limning the Psyche: Explorations in Christian Psychology*, edited by Robert C. Roberts and Mark R. Talbot, 138–64. Grand Rapids: Eerdmans, 1997.

——, ed. *Psychology and Christianity: Five Views*. 2nd. ed. Downers Grove, IL: InterVarsity, 2010.

Johnson, T. Dale, Jr. "Ministry Update: The Association of Certified Biblical Counselors." Biblical Counseling Coalition. July 26, 2021. https://www.biblical counselingcoalition.org/2021/07/26/ministry-update-the-association-of -certified-biblical-counselors/.

Jones, Stanton L. "A Constructive Relationship for Religion with the Science and Profession of Psychology: Perhaps the Boldest Model Yet." *American Psychologist* 49, no. 3 (1994): 184–99.

——. "An Integration Response to Biblical Counseling." In Johnson, *Psychology and Christianity*, 276–81.

——. "An Integration View." In Johnson, *Psychology and Christianity*, 101–28.

——. *Psychology: A Student's Guide*. Wheaton: Crossway, 2014.

Jones, Stanton L., and Richard E. Butman. *Modern Psychotherapies: A Comprehensive Christian Appraisal*. Downers Grove, IL: InterVarsity, 2011.

Kevles, Daniel J. "Eugenics and Human Rights." *BMJ: British Medical Journal* 319, no. 7207 (1999): 435–38.

Kirkpatrick, Lee A. "Toward an Evolutionary Psychology of Religion and Personality." *Journal of Personality* 67, no. 6 (1999): 921–52.

Koch, Sigmund. "The Nature and Limits of Psychological Knowledge: Lessons of a Century qua 'Science.'" *American Psychologist* 36, no. 3 (1985): 257–69.

Koltko-Rivera, Mark. "The Psychology of Worldviews." *Review of General Psychology* 8, no. 1 (2004): 3–58. https://doi.org/10.1037/1089-2680.8.1.3.

Kurzban, Robert, Maxwell N. Burton-Chellew, and Stuart A. West. "The Evolution of Altruism in Humans." *Annual Review of Psychology* 66, no. 1 (2015): 575–99.

Kuyper, Abraham. *Abraham Kuyper: A Centennial Reader*. Edited by James D. Bratt. Grand Rapids: Eerdmans, 1998.

Lambert, Heath. *The Biblical Counseling Movement after Adams*. Wheaton: Crossway, 2011.

——. *A Theology of Biblical Counseling: The Doctrinal Foundations of Counseling Ministry*. Grand Rapids: Zondervan, 2016.

Larmer, Robert A. "Is There Anything Wrong with 'God of the Gaps' Reasoning?" *International Journal for Philosophy of Religion* 52, no. 3 (2002): 129–42.

———. "Psychology, Theism, and Methodological Naturalism." In *Research in the Social Scientific Study of Religion*, vol. 23, edited by Ralph L. Piedmont and David O. Moberg, 135–49. Leiden: Brill, 2012.

Leahey, Thomas Hardy. *A History of Modern Psychology*. 2nd ed. Hoboken, NJ: Prentice Hall, 1994.

Leibniz, Gottfried Wilhelm. "The Principles of Nature and of Grace, Based on Reason." In *Philosophical Papers and Letters*, 2nd ed., edited by Leroy E. Loemker, 636–42. Dordrecht: Kluwer Academic, 1989.

Lewin, Kurt. *A Dynamic Theory of Personality: Selected Papers*. Translated by Donald Keith Adams and Karl E. Zener. Alcester, UK: Read Books Ltd., 2013.

Looy, Heather. "Sex Differences: Evolved, Constructed, and Designed." *Journal of Psychology and Theology* 29, no. 4 (2001): 301–13.

MacArthur, John. "Counseling and the Sinfulness of Humanity." In MacArthur and Mack, *Counseling*, 64–78.

———. "Rediscovering Biblical Counseling." In MacArthur and Mack, *Counseling*, 3–17.

MacArthur, John, and Wayne Mack, eds. *Counseling: How to Counsel Biblically*. Nashville: Nelson, 1994.

Mack, Wayne. "Providing Instruction through Biblical Counseling." In MacArthur and Mack, *Counseling*, 162–75.

MacKay, Donald M. "Brain Research and Human Responsibility." In *Psychology and the Christian Faith: An Introductory Reader*, edited by Stanton L. Jones, 34–50. Grand Rapids: Baker, 1986.

Marshall, Paul. "Overview of Christ and Culture." In *Church and Canadian Culture*, edited by Robert E. Vandervennen, 1–10. Lanham, MD: University Press of America, 1991.

Maslow, A. H. *Toward a Psychology of Being*. New York: Simon & Schuster, 2013.

McFee, Michael R., and Philip G. Monroe. "A Christian Psychology Translation of Emotion-Focused Therapy: Clinical Implications." *Journal of Psychology and Christianity* 30, no. 4 (2011): 317–28.

McLemore, Clinton W. *The Scandal of Psychotherapy: A Guide to Resolving the Tensions between Faith and Counseling*. Carol Stream, IL: Tyndale, 1982.

McRay, Barrett W., Mark A. Yarhouse, and Richard E. Butman. *Modern Psychopathologies: A Comprehensive Christian Appraisal*. 2nd ed. Downers Grove, IL: InterVarsity, 2016.

Moes, Paul, and Donald J. Tellinghuisen. *Exploring Psychology and Christian Faith: An Introductory Guide*. 2nd ed. Grand Rapids: Baker Academic, 2023.

Murphy, Nancey. "Constructing a Radical-Reformation Research Program in Psychology." In *Why Psychology Needs Theology: A Radical-Reformation Perspective*, edited by Alvin Duek and Cameron Lee, 53–78. Grand Rapids: Eerdmans, 2005.

———. "Theological Resources for Integration." In *Why Psychology Needs Theology: A Radical-Reformation Perspective*, edited by Alvin Duek and Cameron Lee, 28–52. Grand Rapids: Eerdmans, 2005.

Murphy, Nancey, and Warren S. Brown. *Did My Neurons Make Me Do It? Philosophical and Neurobiological Perspectives on Moral Responsibility and Free Will*. Oxford: Oxford University Press, 2007.

Myers, David G. "A Levels-of-Explanation Response to Christian Psychology." In Johnson, *Psychology and Christianity*, 179–82.

———. "A Levels-of-Explanation Response to Integration." In Johnson, *Psychology and Christianity*, 129–31.

———. "A Levels-of-Explanation View." In Johnson, *Psychology and Christianity*, 49–78.

Myers, David G., and Malcolm A. Jeeves. *Psychology through the Eyes of Faith*. San Francisco: HarperSanFrancisco, 2002.

Myers, David G., and Letha Dawson Scanzoni. *What God Has Joined Together? The Christian Case for Gay Marriage*. San Francisco: HarperSanFrancisco, 2005.

Nahmias, Eddy. "Why We Have Free Will." *Scientific American* 312, no. 1 (2015): 76–80.

Narramore, Bruce. "Perspectives on the Integration of Psychology and Theology." *Journal of Psychology and Theology* 1, no. 1 (1973): 3–18.

Naugle, David K. *Worldview: The History of a Concept*. Grand Rapids: Eerdmans, 2002.

Nelson, James M. "Missed Opportunities in Dialogue between Psychology and Religion." *Journal of Psychology and Theology* 34, no. 3 (2006): 205–16.

Nelson, James M., and Candice Thomason. "Theistic Psychology: A Patristic Perspective." *Research in the Social Scientific Study of Religion* 23 (2012): 95–106.

Niebuhr, H. Richard. *Christ and Culture*. New York: Harper & Row, 1951.

Peace, Martha. "'Ashley' and Anorexia." In Scott and Lambert, *Counseling the Hard Cases*, 141–70.

Pinker, Steven. "The Evolutionary Psychology of Religion." Speech at the annual meeting of the Freedom from Religion Foundation. Madison, WI. October 29, 2004. https://ffrf.org/outreach/awards/emperor-has-no-clothes-award/item/20327-steven-pinker.

———. "Science Is Not Your Enemy." *New Republic* 244, no. 13 (2013). https://newrepublic.com/article/114127/science-not-enemy-humanities.

Ponterotto, Joseph G. "Qualitative Research in Counseling Psychology: A Primer on Research Paradigms and Philosophy of Science." *Journal of Counseling Psychology* 52, no. 2 (2005): 126–36.

Porter, Richard J. "The Biopsychosocial Model in Mental Health." *Australian & New Zealand Journal of Psychiatry* 54, no. 8 (2020): 773–74.

Powlison, David. *The Biblical Counseling Movement: History and Context.* Greensboro, NC: New Growth Press, 2010.

———. "A Biblical Counseling View." In Johnson, *Psychology and Christianity*, 245–73.

———. "Idols of the Heart and 'Vanity Fair.'" *Journal of Biblical Counseling* 13, no. 2 (1995): 35–50.

Rasmussen, Kyler R., Madelynn Stackhouse, Susan D. Boon, Karly Comstock, and Rachel Ross. "Meta-Analytic Connections between Forgiveness and Health: The Moderating Effects of Forgiveness-Related Distinctions." *Psychology & Health* 34, no. 5 (2019): 515–34.

Rennie, David L. "Two Thoughts on Abraham Maslow." *Journal of Humanistic Psychology* 48, no. 4 (2008): 445–48.

Ringdahl, Joel E., Todd Kopelman, and Terry S. Falcomata. "Applied Behavior Analysis and Its Application to Autism and Autism Related Disorders." In *Applied Behavior Analysis for Children with Autism Spectrum Disorders*, edited by Johnny Matson, 15–32. New York: Springer, 2009.

Roberts, Robert C. "Emotion and the Fruit of the Spirit." In *Psychology and the Christian Faith: An Introductory Reader*, edited by Stanton L. Jones, 78–94. Grand Rapids: Baker, 1986.

———. "Outline of Pauline Psychotherapy." In *Care for the Soul*, edited by Mark R. McMinn and Timothy R. Phillips, 134–63. Downers Grove, IL: InterVarsity, 2001.

———. *Taking the World to Heart: Self and Other in an Age of Therapies*. Grand Rapids: Eerdmans, 1993.

Robinson, Paul A., and Paul W. Robinson. *Freud and His Critics*. Berkeley: University of California Press, 1993.

Rogers, Carl. *Client-Centered Therapy: Its Current Practice, Implications, and Theory*. Boston: Houghton Mifflin, 1951.

Schultz, Duane P., and Sydney Ellen Schultz. *A History of Modern Psychology*. 7th ed. San Diego: Harcourt, 2000.

Schwartz, Renee, and Norman Lederman. "What Scientists Say: Scientists' Views of Nature of Science and Relation to Science Context." *International Journal of Science Education* 30, no. 6 (2008): 727–71.

Scott, Stuart, and Heath Lambert., eds. *Counseling the Hard Cases: True Stories Illustrating the Sufficiency of God's Resources in Scripture*. Nashville: B&H, 2012.

Seligman, Martin E. P., Peter Railton, Roy F. Baumeister, and Chandra Sripada. "Navigating into the Future or Driven by the Past." *Perspectives on Psychological Science* 8, no. 2 (2013): 119–41.

Shackelford, Todd K., and James R. Liddle. "Understanding the Mind from an Evolutionary Perspective: An Overview of Evolutionary Psychology." *Wiley Interdisciplinary Reviews: Cognitive Science* 5, no. 3 (2014): 247–60.

Silverman, Kenneth, August F. Holtyn, and Forrest Toegel. "The Utility of Operant Conditioning to Address Poverty and Drug Addiction." *Perspectives on Behavior Science* 42, no. 3 (2019): 525–46.

Skinner, B. F. *Beyond Freedom and Dignity*. New York: Knopf, 1971.

———. *Learning and Behavior: What Makes Us Human*. Directed and narrated by Charles Collingwood. Produced by Michael Sklar. New York: Carousel Film & Video, 1959. https://archive.org/details/bf-skinner-learning-and -behavior-1959.

———. *Reflections on Behaviorism and Society*. Hoboken, NJ: Prentice Hall, 1978.

———. *Walden Two*. Indianapolis: Hackett, 2005.

———. "Why I Am Not a Cognitive Psychologist." *Behaviorism* 5, no. 2 (1977): 1–10.

Slife, Brent D., and Jeffrey S. Reber. "Against Methodological Confinement: Toward a Pluralism of Methods and Interpretations." *Psychology of Religion and Spirituality* 13, no. 1 (2021): 14.

Smith, David I. *Learning from the Stranger: Christian Faith and Cultural Diversity*. Grand Rapids: Eerdmans, 2009.

Smith, Gregory A. "About Three-in-Ten US Adults Are Now Religiously Unaffiliated." Pew Research Center. December 14, 2021. https://www.pewresearch .org/religion/2021/12/14/about-three-in-ten-u-s-adults-are-now-religiously -unaffiliated/.

Smith, Noel W. *Current Systems in Psychology: History, Theory, Research, and Applications*. Perth, Australia: Wadsworth, 2001.

Staddon, John E. R., and Daniel T. Cerutti. "Operant Conditioning." *Annual Review of Psychology* 54 (2003): 115–44.

Strawn, Brad D., and Warren S. Brown. *Enhancing Christian Life: How Extended Cognition Augments Religious Community*. Downers Grove, IL: InterVarsity, 2020.

Stump, James B. "Non-Reductive Physicalism—A Dissenting Voice." *Christian Scholar's Review* 36, no. 1 (2006): 63–76.

Sulloway, Frank J. *Freud, Biologist of the Mind: Beyond the Psychoanalytic Legend*. Cambridge, MA: Harvard University Press, 1992.

Tjeltveit, Alan C. "Lost Opportunities, Partial Successes, and Key Questions: Some Historical Lessons." *Journal of Psychology and Theology* 40, no. 1 (2012): 16–20.

Vanhoozer, Kevin J. "The Sufficiency of Scripture: A Critical and Constructive Account." *Journal of Psychology and Theology* 49, no. 3 (2021): 218–34.

Van Leeuwen, Mary Stewart. *The Sorcerer's Apprentice: A Christian Looks at the Changing Face of Psychology*. Downers Grove, IL: InterVarsity, 1982.

Vawter, Bruce. "Original Sin." In *The Westminster Dictionary of Christian Theology*, edited by Alan Richardson and John Bowden, 420–21. Louisville: Westminster John Knox, 1983.

Veenhof, Jan. "Nature and Grace in Bavinck." *Pro Rege* 34, no. 4 (2006): 10–31.

Vidal, Clément. "What Is a Worldview?" In *Nieuwheid denken. De wetenschappen enhet creatieve aspect van de werkelijkheid*, edited by H. Van Belle and J. Van der Veken, 71–85. Leuven, Belgium: ACCO, 2008.

Vitz, Paul C. *Psychology as Religion: The Cult of Self-Worship*. Grand Rapids: Eerdmans, 1994.

Wakefield, Jerome C. "Diagnostic Issues and Controversies in DSM-5: Return of the False Positives Problem." *Annual Review of Clinical Psychology* 12 (2016): 105–32.

Ward, Steven. "Filling the World with Self-esteem: A Social History of Truth-Making." *Canadian Journal of Sociology / Cahiers canadiens de sociologie* (1996): 1–23.

Watson, John B. *Behaviorism*. 1924. Reprint, New York: Routledge, 1998.

Watson, John B., and Rosalie Rayner. "Conditioned Emotional Reactions." *Journal of Experimental Psychology* 3, no. 1 (1920): 1–14.

Watson, P. J. "Faithful Translation and Postmodernism: Norms and Linguistic Relativity within a Christian Ideological Surround." *Edification* 2, no. 1 (2008): 5–18.

Wax, Trevin. "3 Reasons We Need Today's Anabaptists." The Gospel Coalition. February 6, 2017. https://www.thegospelcoalition.org/blogs/trevin -wax/3-reasons-we-need-todays-anabaptists/.

Welch, Edward T. *Blame It on the Brain? Distinguishing Chemical Imbalances, Brain Disorders, and Disobedience.* Greensboro, NC: New Growth, 2012.

Wicket, Dan. "'Mary' and Paralyzing Fear." In Scott and Lambert, *Counseling the Hard Cases*, 111–40.

Wilson, Edward O. "The Biological Basis of Morality." *Atlantic Monthly* 281, no. 4 (1998). https://www.theatlantic.com/magazine/archive/1998/04/the -biological-basis-of-morality/377087/.

Witte, John, Jr. *Law and Protestantism: The Legal Teachings of the Lutheran Reformation.* Cambridge: Cambridge University Press, 2002.

Wolters, Albert M. *Creation Regained: Biblical Basics for a Reformational Worldview.* Grand Rapids: Eerdmans, 2005.

Wood, Adam. "Disembodied Souls without Dualism: Thomas Aquinas on Why You Won't Go to Heaven When You Die (but Your Soul Just Might)." *Christian Scholar's Review* 49, no. 3 (2020): 215–30.

Worthington, Everett L., Jr. *Coming to Peace with Psychology: What Christians Can Learn from Psychological Science.* Downers Grove, IL: InterVarsity, 2013.

Wright, N. T. "Mind, Spirit, Soul and Body: All for One and One for All— Reflections on Paul's Anthropology in His Complex Contexts." In *Pauline Perspectives: Essays on Paul, 1978–2013*, 455–73. Minneapolis: Fortress, 2013.

Index

actions vs. events, 133–34, 135–36
Adams, Jay, 90, 91–92, 93–94, 99, 102–3
agency
  biblical reductionist views of, 101
  in humanizer model, 130, 132–35, 138,
    140, 142
  human nature and, 23–27, 29, 30–31
  in psychology, 33, 40, 46, 80, 83, 134–35,
    156
  in religion, 17–18, 29, 30–31, 63–64, 160
agents vs. non-agents, 133–34
aggression, 37, 38, 112
Anabaptists, 57, 58, 62, 63
anthropology, 9, 28–31, 82, 158
applied behavior analysis, 40n18
Aquinas, 52
Association of Biblical Counselors, 90–91
Association of Certified Biblical Counselors,
  93n15
Atienza, Mercedes, 154–55
axiology, 9, 23, 25, 27–28, 36, 82, 150–52

Bavinck, Herman, 51, 58, 60–61, 97
behavior, human
  vs. events, 133–34, 135–36
  in evolutionary psychology, 78
  in humanizer model, 130, 135–37, 138–42
behavioral neuroscience, 44–45
behaviorism, 39–41, 75–77, 83, 88
Bendroth, Margaret, 59
biblical counseling, 90–103

biblical reductionism. *See* reductionism,
  biblical
biblical translation, 157–58, 159
biopsychosocial model of psychology, 101
Blame It on the Brain? (Welch), 94–95
body-soul dualism. *See* dualism
brain function, 20, 154–56, 157
brokenness, 29, 30, 63
Brown, Warren, 21, 30

Cahalan, Kathleen, 149, 151
calling, 151
Calvin, John, 60, 62
Cantero, Jose, 154–55
Carson, Donald, 54, 55–56, 58, 61, 62
Carter, John, 69, 121
Christ, sovereignty of, 61, 99n32, 116
Christ-culture views, 54–55, 56–57, 59–
  62, 97, 119, 144
Christian church
  disunity within, 49–51
  perceived threats to, 93
  relationships of, 55–56, 57–58, 59, 60–62
  See also specific churches and movements
Christian Counseling and Education Foun-
  dation (CCEF), 89
Christian Psychology, 130, 138–42,
  144–45
Christian worldview
  biblical reductionism and, 97–98
  in Christian Psychology, 139, 140, 141

175